Changing the View

Changing the View

Student-Led Parent Conferences

Terri Austin

HEINEMANN
Portsmouth, NH

Heinemann
A division of Reed Elsevier Inc.
361 Hanover Street
Portsmouth, NH 03801-3912
Offices and agents throughout the world

Every effort has been made to contact the copyright holders for permission to reprint borrowed material where necessary. We regret any oversights that may have occurred and would be happy to rectify them in future printings of this work.

Library of Congress Cataloging-in-Publication Data

Austin, Terri.
    Changing the view : student-led parent conferences / Terri Austin.
      p.   cm.
    Includes bibliographical references.
    ISBN 0-435-08818-1 (acid-free paper)
    1. Parent-teacher conferences—Alaska—Fairbanks Area—Case studies.   2. Interaction analysis in education—Case studies.
3. Students—Alaska—Fairbanks Area—Rating of—Case studies.
I. Title.
LC225.5.A88   1994
371.1'03—dc20   94-21497
                                             CIP

Editor: Carolyn Coman
Production: Renée M. Pinard
Cover design: Darci Mehall

Printed in the United States of America on acid-free paper
99 98 97 96 95 94 EB 1 2 3 4 5 6 7 8 9

Contents

ACKNOWLEDGMENTS   vii

INTRODUCTION   *Changing the View*   1

CHAPTER ONE   *Setting Directions, Building Relationships*   7

CHAPTER TWO   *Growing in Confidence and Voice*   27

CHAPTER THREE   *The Main Event: The Student-Parent Conference*   65

CHAPTER FOUR   *Celebrating the Process, Taking the Next Step*   75

CHAPTER FIVE   *Reflections*   85

CHAPTER SIX   *Final Notes on Management: Fitting the Pieces Together*   89

BIBLIOGRAPHY   105

Acknowledgments

Alaska is an incredibly beautiful place to live. In the winter, the northern lights dance in the sky, and in the summer, the sun fills entire days. But underneath all the beauty lies a land full of challenges—extreme temperatures, long periods of darkness, feelings of isolation from the rest of the world. To survive, we've learned to work with and rely on each other. This book is really a reflection of Alaskan cooperation and creativity; it belongs to many people. I just happened to write it down. Without these people, I wouldn't have begun:

- My students and their parents, who eagerly joined me in the discovery process and willingly shared their insights and observations. They were my partners in research.
- My coresearchers in the Alaska Teacher Research Network, who rejoiced and encouraged me all along the way. Special appreciation goes to Janelle McCracken, who set deadlines, and for Scott Christian, who prodded at just the right time.
- My principal, Patricia Baker-Benally, who offered me the freedom and support to explore new areas.
- All the teachers who visited the classroom or asked about student-parent conferences. Every time we talked, I learned something new.
- Dawn Boyer and Carolyn Coman at Heinemann, who patiently worked with me all along the way.

Special thanks go to Ruth Hubbard. Her enthusiasm, confidence, and faith propelled me forward into arenas I've never dreamed of.

My deepest appreciation and thanks go to Shirley Kaltenbach, my sister in research. Together we go where neither of us alone would ever venture. She's given me friendship, knowledge, and courage. For all of those things, I am deeply grateful.

Finally, how can I ever begin to thank my husband, Ken? He's been my most ardent supporter. He's edited my writing, fielded my phone calls, wiped my tears, and cooked my meals. Most of all, he's given me the gifts of time and love.

The real voyage of discovery consists not in seeking new landscapes but in having new eyes.

Proust

Introduction:
Changing the View

Out in the hall standing by the lockers, sixth-grade students discuss report cards: "What did she give you?" "She always gets good grades." "My parent-teacher conference is today. I hope my mom forgets. I'll probably get in trouble tonight if she does come."

I heard comments like these four times a year for nine years. My sixth graders are like sixth graders everywhere, concerned with clothes, music, and friends and very vocal in expressing their opinions about grades. My students and I work together in a 182-pupil school located on a military post right outside Fairbanks, Alaska. The student population is a delightful mix of ethnic backgrounds—Asian, Hispanic, Black, and Caucasian—and since it's not unusual for families to be a blend of cultures, many speak more than one language. Another aspect of a military community is the predominance of two-parent families, although many are combination families that include stepfathers and stepmothers, half brothers and half sisters, and occasionally members of the extended family. Like any other classroom, the ability range of students is wide and varied. Here, the support staff (such as the reading teacher, bilingual aide, and special education teachers) come into the classroom to work with students rather than students leaving to see them. Due to the military rotation schedule, by the time my students come to me they've usually attended about five different schools scattered all over the world. The traveling has made them wonderfully adaptable to almost any situation. They all know what it's like to be the "new kid" and accept the rotation of students in and out of the classroom as part of the normal routine. Welcoming celebrations and good-bye parties are commonly scheduled events in the room.

Grades were also common "events" in my classroom. The students graded all their own work, so they were aware of their grades in each subject. Tests were returned promptly and reviewed in class. All papers were examined and were required to be taken home. But at the end of each quarter, the marks on the report card came as a complete surprise to many students. My students saw no relationship between effort, study habits, and participation to the grades printed on their report cards. I felt like there were two parts to each student. One part was the active, interested learner that participated in all aspects of the class-room and had lots to say about everything. The other part was the passive student who accepted the report card as a final judgment given by an all-knowing teacher. No matter what I did, students viewed grades as something that I gave them, not something that reflected their efforts and learning. If anything, I believed that students thought a Grade Card Fairy randomly sprinkled grades over the stack of report cards at the end of each quarter. This mildly disturbed me in the begin-ning years of teaching, but as I moved closer and closer to a child-centered process classroom, I found this whole attitude toward report cards and grading more and more disturbing.

I thought back to my elementary years and remembered my feeling of dread when my mother attended parent conferences. I realize now that I was a pretty good student, but then I never knew that. I always wondered what bad things the teacher was saying about me and if I would pass on to the next grade. I was like the students in my room. I had no knowledge of the assessment process, and I had no real concept of myself as a learner. As I thought more about this, I realized there were three main issues to the problem.

First, the students accepted no responsibility for their learning. Again, it was something *done* to them, not something they did for themselves. As I continued to teach, I was increasingly seeing compla-cent students with an attitude of "just tell me what I have to do, then leave me alone." I wanted student involvement but wasn't seeing any interest.

Second, I totally controlled the assessment process. I wanted stu-dents to assume responsibility, but I was not allowing that to happen. I worked very hard to establish a community of learners where we all learn together. I don't work behind an official "teacher" desk but have a student desk arranged within a group of other student desks to help me become a working member of the class. I took pride in the fact that we were a process classroom where we worked and solved problems together. There was a feeling of "us." But an interesting thing happened when report-card time came. I found myself physically moving from my student desk among the students to my "big desk" (Atwell 1987) at the front of the room. It was like a barrier suddenly separated us. Now the feeling within the class was "me and them." We were no longer "us."

The third issue was that of parent contact. To be truthful, parent contact was very minimal and, in the beginning of my teacher career, I wanted it that way. I wanted parents to agree with what I was doing and not ask a lot of questions. In the journey toward a process classroom, I realized that parent involvement is essential. In my district, report cards are issued every nine weeks, which is four times a year. During the first and third quarters, parents are given an assigned time for a teacher conference. Fifteen minutes are scheduled for each parent. Usually the parents sit outside the door waiting for their turn. I go to the door, invite them in, show them the report card, and make a few comments. The parent nods, signs, and leaves before the next parent comes in. The parents then would go home and translate what I said to the student. As a result, I saw little long-term student improvement. Some students did try for a day or so, but very few students sustained their effort.

Within all three of these issues, the unifying thread was my control. I was in control of every situation. I wanted students to accept more responsibility, but I never gave them a chance to practice it. I wanted students to care about grades, but I never included them in the assessment process. I wanted more parent involvement, but I never offered opportunities for them to join the class. As Nancie Atwell (1987) says, I "orchestrated" everything.

At the same time I was becoming aware of these issues, my school counselor showed me a small article about two British Columbian teachers who had their students leading their own parent conferences. That same year, I had a difficult class of sixth graders. Physical violence, verbal abuse, and learning apathy were always close the surface of any activity. I figured I had nothing to lose if I had the students give this approach a try. I told the students they would be sitting down with their parents and explaining their report card. With just that limited action, I was amazed at the difference in them. Usually the last quarter of the school year is not a good one for students. In April and May, the lengthening sun-filled days entice students to stay up well past normal bedtimes and play outside later in the evenings. After the long winter months of darkness, it's hard to resist the sunshine and blue sky, and so school often becomes something that is done in between periods of being outside. Little homework is completed and talk centers around evening activities. But when the students realized they were the ones sharing their work and report cards to their parents, their attitude changed. They took an interest in their work and some showed more effort than they had all year. I figured I had something here, but I needed to think this whole process through carefully.

Over the summer I talked with other educators and did extensive reading. To the simple concept of students leading their own conferences, I added Patrick Dias' (1989) ideas of valuing student voices and offering student responsibility. He also talks about "the importance of the journey, not the destination." It's easy for teachers to be tour directors, and I was a very good one. I planned the trip, I told students what to pack, I ushered them on the plane, and I told them what to look at. When we deplaned, I asked them what they learned. Basically they learned very little because I controlled every aspect of their learning.

Along with being the ultimate tour director, I also continued to make assumptions about their learning. By only looking at tests I decided whether or not they were learning. I wasn't doing this with their writing, however. Following the advice of Donald Graves, Nancie Atwell, and other writing-instruction theorists, I met with students on a regular basis and asked them about their writing. I wanted to know what they knew, so in individual conferences the students and I discussed what they were attempting to do and what they felt they successfully accomplished. I soon realized that I could use this same concept for all subjects, not just writing. If I wanted to know what students really knew, I needed to ask them, not make assumptions for them.

Another assumption that I was making was that learning takes place at school. I knew, of course, that learning takes place everywhere, but I felt the really significant learning happened at school within the classroom under my direction. I read Taylor and Dorsey-Gaines' (1988) work that examined the learning that takes place in any home environment. It was exactly what I needed to help me broaden my view of "significant" learning.

The next important piece of my thinking was filled in by Terry Johnson (1989). In a workshop on assessment, he talked about the importance of knowing community values and then somehow meshing those values with the values of the classroom. Kathryn Au (Kamehameha Elementary School, Honolulu) successfully combined community values and school values when she changed her emphasis from a written response to reading to an oral response. She states in the conclusion of her study that

> In the case of Hawaiian students, talk story is a particularly significant nonschool speech event with group performance being an important value. . . . It seems important, then, for teachers working with young, culturally different students to be aware of the different values which may underlie different ways of speaking. (1985, p. 411)

In the rural communities of Alaska, cooperation among individuals is essential for survival. By building on Johnson's idea of meshing values (1989), schools support cooperative learning rather than stress individual competition. Following these examples, I saw that if I could identify the community values and then incorporate them into what I value as an instructor, then the student would be in a better position to be successful in school.

And so the students and I began a journey. We tried a variety of ways to incorporate the ideas of Dias, Graves, Taylor, and Johnson. After each student-led conference, we would sit down and talk about what worked and what didn't. I've found this journey's process continually changes; the ideas in this book represent where we just were. The students and I invite you to join us as we describe our adventure together.

Setting Directions, Building Relationships

1

My mother is a dressmaker and I grew up playing with scraps of material, scissors, and pins. As I constructed doll clothes, I practiced using a needle and thread by sewing on snaps and buttons. Mom and I often spent Saturdays in fabric shops examining material and choosing patterns. She made all of my clothes and, when I was about six, she let me begin choosing the material and patterns she would use for them. At the age of nine, I made my first dress. It was of blue cotton with a pattern of smiling gray kittens. It had fourteen tiny tucks down the front and, frustrated by trying to stitch in straight lines, I ripped out this section a lot. But what I most remember about the dress is the feeling of pride when I wore it for the first time. I had experienced success with my first sewing project because I was ready. I had watched my mother sew. I was familiar with the tools. I knew the vocabulary. Most of all, my mother had believed in me; she showed her faith by letting me sew a real dress.

I've found that student-led conferences require this type of context and preparation. They are not something that can be introduced a week before the quarter ends. The success of the conferences depends upon extensive background preparation. I lived in an atmosphere of sewing and was introduced to the idea long before my first individual project. Students and parents need a similar introduction. It's important for them to hear terms like *portfolio* and *reflection* as a natural part of classroom vocabulary. I must provide, as my mother did, an environment that allows the students to become familiar with the tools and the language of conferences. The students should have the opportunity to experiment with oral discussions, figuring out their best strategy in expressing themselves. The students need time to practice with these elements. I have to have faith in my students, as my mother did in me, that they will know how to conduct student-parent conferences.

In reflecting back on the last six years of student-parent conferences, I believe there are three concepts necessary for their success: a classroom community needs to be developed, communication must be established, and relationships have to be built.

Developing a Classroom Community

As soon as I obtain my class list, I work toward my goal of creating a classroom community where everyone feels comfortable taking risks, where students help each other, and where we value others enough to learn from and with them. Weaver (1990) points out that "People do not engage or invest themselves in learning tasks that they perceive as threatening to their self-esteem" (10). So if I want my students to learn and be actively involved, I must create a nonthreatening environment for each child. I begin before school starts in August and continue throughout the year using cooperative learning and the process approach to learning to provide the foundation of the community.

Beginnings

Communication through personal contact and letters set the pattern for the year. By the time students arrive on the first day, they have already received a letter and a home visit from me (see Fig. 1–1).

As the students enter the room on the first day, there is another letter on their desk welcoming them to the room and telling them how glad I am that they are part of the class. These letters reaffirm the positive aspects of being in the class and also provide a point of contact to any last-minute new student (see Fig. 1–2). The letters are individually handwritten, brief, and vary in content. These letters are important because they set the tone and model the interaction pattern the students and I continue throughout the year.

On the first day, I see my job as modeling all the positive elements involved in classroom life. I participate in every activity. I get out from behind the big desk (Atwell 1987) and interact with the students as a member of the learning community. I model sharing by asking to borrow a ruler or crayons. I ask for opinions from the student beside me. I ask how to spell a word. I work from a student desk placed among other student desks, which by itself moves me into the learning community more than anything else I have done. It's not me and them;

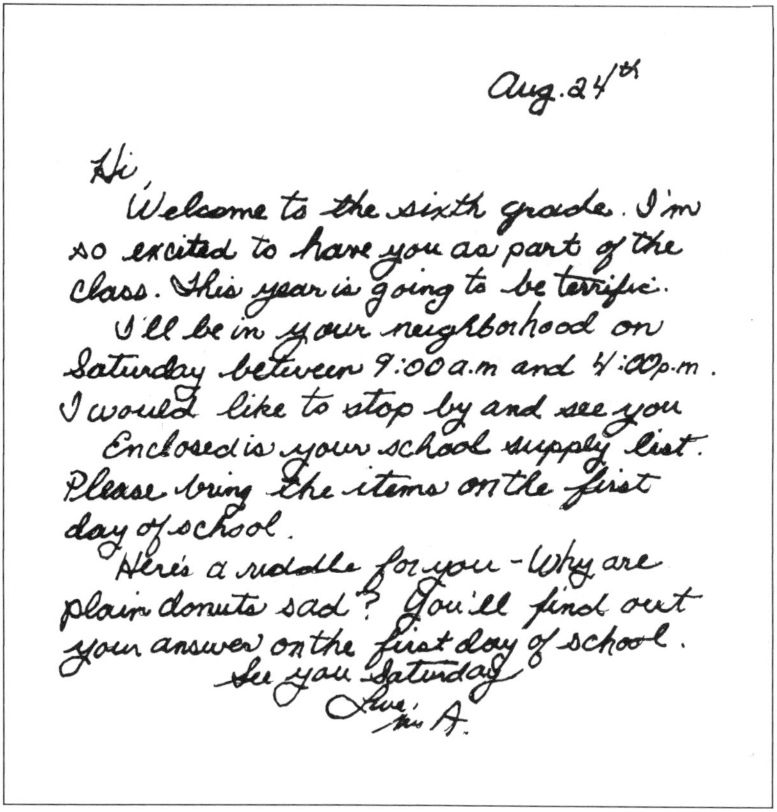

> Aug. 24th
>
> Hi,
> Welcome to the sixth grade. I'm so excited to have you as part of the class. This year is going to be terrific.
> I'll be in your neighborhood on Saturday between 9:00 a.m and 4:00 p.m. I would like to stop by and see you.
> Enclosed is your school supply list. Please bring the items on the first day of school.
> Here's a riddle for you – Why are plain donuts sad? You'll find out your answer on the first day of school.
> See you Saturday
> Love,
> Mrs. A.

FIGURE 1–1

it is us. I am a member of the group—a mature member, but still an active, working member (Dewey 1938). This again sets the stage for all future interaction where we talk and discuss, solve problems, and learn together.

I use many activities to build unity the first few months of school. Some are subtle and others are more direct. A very subtle one, at least to the students, involves my choice of pronouns. During this beginning period, I'm very aware of using collective pronouns such as *we, our,* and *us.* "Our" books need to be picked up. "We" need to line up. It's time for "us" to begin. What do you think "we" should do? This repeated message continually tells the students that they are part of a group. When students begin using collective pronouns in speech or in journals, I know they've grasped the sense of community. In Jennifer's journal (Fig. 1–3), she discusses an art project where we made fish.

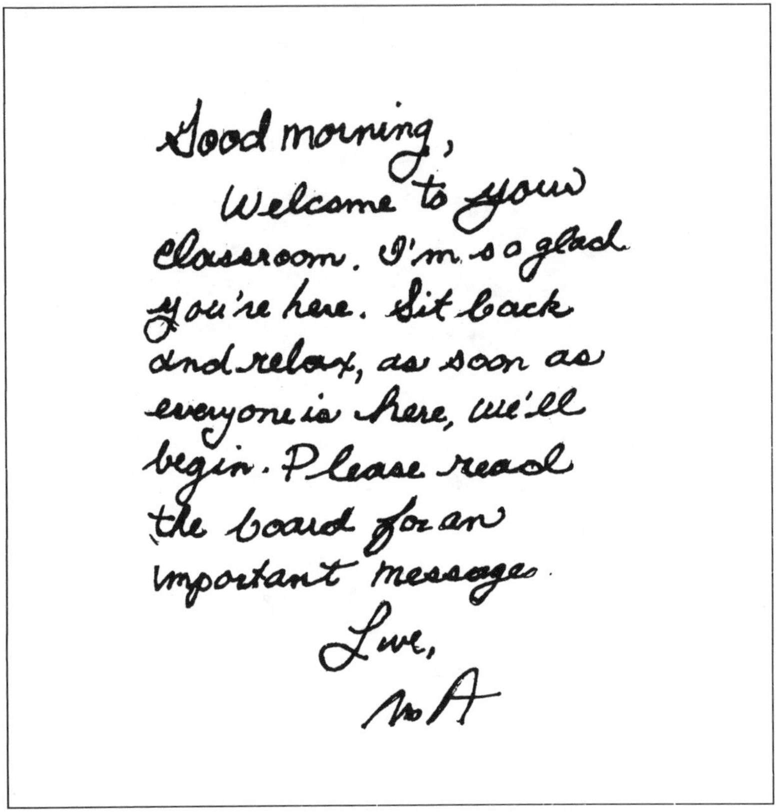

Good morning,
Welcome to your classroom. I'm so glad you're here. Sit back and relax, as soon as everyone is here, we'll begin. Please read the board for an important message.
Love,
Mrs. A

FIGURE 1–2

Her use of pronouns shows her feeling of belonging to the class community. I've found that if I want the class to become a family I must express myself in such a way as to reflect this belief.

Other ways I build a sense of community early in the year are through a class project, a class goal, and a class celebration. All three pull students together and allow them to see themselves as members of a successful group.

I usually begin with the development of a group project of some type. Sometime during September, my class creates a class name and logo. In the last three years, we have been Raiders of Lost Knowledge, Students of the Midnight Sun, and Ultra As. We paint our motto and logo on our school sweatshirts. We wear these every Friday to develop a sense of ownership and belonging. Other projects have included producing plays, publishing class books, and sharing food at potluck lunches.

Journal Date October 16

Today we had art classes and we made sea animals using patterns. It was a lot of fun. We have a lot of creative people in our class.

Jennifer,
I agree. I think you are one of them. Love, Mrs. A

FIGURE 1–3

Group goals also create a sense of community. One year, early in my teaching career, my class had the opportunity to work with a nationally known dance company visiting schools in Alaska. After one full day of practice, we presented a show complete with strobe and blackout lights, jazz, and costumes. During those two days, I saw incredible things happen to my students. Ron, the outcast of my class, suddenly gained importance because he was the pivotal man in the pyramid routine. Larry and Sharon, the shiest and most withdrawn students, were flinging themselves across the stage and encouraging others to do the same. Self-confidence and pride enveloped every student for weeks afterwards. After watching this phenomena, it struck me that I could create this type of happening on my own and that I needed to do it early in the year.

I call these happenings "magic moments" because they truly are amazing. They excite the group and require work by every member of the class for success. Moorman and Dishon (1983) point out that the more difficult the goal, the stronger the unity will be within the group once the goal is reached. Blake, Mouton, and Allen (1987) reinforce this idea.

> When people are able to grapple with a difficult and complex problem and come out of it with something far better than could have been had without the joint effort, the emotional reaction is one of deep satisfaction. There is something at the very core of human experience that finds gratification from that kind of performance. Those involved have not only proved it can be done, but also that they can do it. It reinforces a person's feelings of self-value and creates a willingness among people to be mutually supportive of one another in future efforts. (9)

For all of these reasons, I plan the first project very carefully. It's important that the task not be overwhelming, though it must provide an interesting challenge. It must require every student to participate for us to reach our goal. And, most important, every student needs to feel successful. I examine my class carefully before proposing a project. Each class has a strength, and one of my first goals is to identify and try to build on that class strength. One year, my class was very artistic. Many students took dancing, art, and music lessons. Several were very creative writers. As an initial project, the class produced an evening of music, poetry, and an original play for the community.

I found that with sixth graders an outside audience is a very important aspect of the project. First, because there is a "real" audience involved, I can remove myself from that traditional position of judge into a position of participant. And second, the audience increases the desire of the students to succeed. We've performed plays for the community, set up a mini–science fair for other classes, cooked a complete dinner with our families as guests, and painted the entire gym one year for the school.

Once we accomplish our goal, we celebrate together, which is my third way of building classroom community at the beginning of the year. The celebration can be anything from awards (participation certificates) to having a party. It's not how elaborate the celebration is that matters so much as that we celebrate. During the celebration we discuss what it feels like to be successful. As we talk about the importance of each member of the class, we also show respect and appreciation for everyone's participation. After the dance production, it was important for Ron to hear praise from others and it was equally important for his peers to hear him being praised. It was then that others began changing their opinions about him. As Johnson and Johnson (1987) point out, "Being part of a team effort results in feelings of camaraderie, belonging, and pride. Feelings of success are shared and pride is taken in other's accomplishments as well as one's own" (28). The celebration allows us to cement those feelings by openly talking about them. Toward the end of the celebration, we talk about what we would change if we had the chance to do it again. My purpose is to create a setting where students begin to reflect on their involvement and the importance of their role in the success of the project.

I value this part of the project as much as the project itself because it provides an opportunity for students to hear how others approach the reflective process. They are also learning how to make a constuctive assessment of their own actions. This practice will help them as they begin to prepare for their student-parent conference.

Valuing Each Other

The large project bonds students together and, through active participation, we learn a lot about each other. In the first month of school, we learn each other's phone numbers in case we need help. We call each other for help with homework or to let others know we won't be at school the next day. It's difficult to work with people when names are not known, so we learn and accurately spell everyone's name. We make neighborhood maps to locate classmates in case we have to work together outside of school. By the end of the month, each student has had the opportunity to work with every other class member, either as a partner or within a small group. One beneficial side effect of this process is that as students work together in successful situations, their negative perceptions of each other begin to disappear. They begin to see the positive aspects in fellow students and start to value them as individuals.

An initial step in learning to value involves learning to praise. With sixth graders, put-downs are a common form of interaction. Within the first week of school, we brainstorm "praise phrases." Together we compile a list that usually includes a mixture of current slang and traditional courtesies (see Fig. 1–4).

Displayed in the room for reference, these words provide a beginning vocabulary for making a positive statement. As the year progresses, we refine the vocabulary to fit the task. Phrases also develop special meaning as the class grows closer together and relationships develop.

Class Meeting

Part of the process of learning to value each other is the development of careful listening habits and respectful attention to opinions. Class meetings provide continual practice and consistent reinforcement of these skills. The class meeting is a place where problems can be discussed and solutions sought. It's also a place to discuss new projects and the agenda for the coming month. Finally, it's a comfortable place to just get together and see how everyone is doing. The rules are simple: take turns, don't interrupt anyone, and accept all ideas.

I feel it's important that the students learn to deal with issues that affect the class as a whole. If we are a family, then we must face problems openly and work together to find a solution.

The meetings also set a tone of honesty and concern for the class as a whole. The students have to be honest if they are bringing up a problem to discuss. The problem has to be genuine. Boasts, lies, and exaggerations are easily seen by everyone. The meeting is not a place to vent personal problems but a place to discuss problems that involve the whole class. Through problem identification and problem solving, the students extend themselves and assume responsibility for our classroom family's issues. I want them to see themselves as part of a caring group of people who will help those in need. We all support each other so we all can succeed.

Our meetings also provide a genuine arena for oral discussion. Students become familiar with speaking to a larger audience. They try out ways of addressing others and the means of clearly expressing

Looking good

Out of this world

You're number 1

Awesome

Nice work

Supreme

wouzers

unreal

1st rate

way-to-go

Perfect

helpful

fantastic

Jolly Good Job

very kind

Great Job

Cool

wowie zow zow

FIGURE 1–4

opinions. During the student-parent conference, the student draws on this public-speaking experience. In the discussions, the students hear many possible solutions. For numerous students, this is the first time they encounter the real-world situation of no one right answer. They see flexibility in problem solving. These discussions provide a type of modeling for students that they can use in the reflection stage of the conference process.

Process Classroom

The word *process* implies movement and action, which is exactly what a process classroom builds upon. It's a classroom where the process of learning is valued and examined by the members of the learning community. The product is still at the end, but the path to the end product is just as valuable as the "goal." In the summer of 1989, Patrick Dias was a guest presenter in a whole language class I was facilitating. He said that by always making decisions for students, teachers have the student "arrive without having traveled." That picture stayed with me for a long time. In a process classroom, the journey is just as important as the destination. The students and teacher are traveling companions who together plot the course, travel the same roads, pause at scenic sites, and share perceptions and experiences.

Cooperative Learning

Cooperative learning is the other foundation stone of my classroom. The students become so accustomed to working together in small groups, with partners, and in large groups that cooperation with peers becomes a natural and expected part of the day. Goodlad (1984) addressed the problem of student passivity. His premise is that students have been taught to sit back, watch, and wait—to be spectators rather than active participants. I want my students to be involved, supportive learners. I want them to cook the meal and eat the dinner, not just read the menu. Cooperative learning provides the structure for this transition.

Faith and Trust

Covey (1989) states, "If there is little or no trust there is no foundation for permanent success" (21). Trust and faith reinforce the success felt during the cooperation activities. I need to consistently show students that I have faith that they will learn and that I trust them. As I repeatedly model these attitudes to students, they begin to internalize them and grow to fit the expectations.

On the first day of school, I discuss trust. I tell students that I trust them to do what is expected: I trust them to monitor themselves; I trust them to work hard; I trust them to do their homework; I trust them to be kind to each other; and I trust them to tell the truth. The students grade their own papers because I feel it's important for them to see what mistakes they are making. I trust them to be honest when doing this. I expect students to tell me when they don't have an assignment. I expect them to be as honest with me as I am honest with them. In learning to be honest with me, they learn how to be honest with themselves. If they are to be successful assessors of their learning, they need to know how to internalize all of these behaviors.

Reflective Learners

To be successful in assessing their learning, students need to be aware of their actions during the stages of problem solving. By consistently providing time within the school day for the students to think back on the activity just completed and to critically assess the learning task or problem and their role, the students can effectively learn to self-evaluate. Through language they have the capability to be the subjects and objects of their own behavior (Vygotsky 1978). Students assume the role of assessors, looking into themselves and not to me.

Graves (1983) states that growth comes when problems are solved. I want my students to be deeply involved in all aspects of problem solving and to dig below the surface of assignments. By taking the time to reflect on a completed activity, students become aware of their obstacles and possible actions to overcome them. The reflection process adds another layer of self-esteem as learners realize they can solve problems, as well as adding to personal knowledge about being a learner.

Often I'll ask the class to do a reflective fastwrite in their metacognition journals. The term fastwrite is rough draft writing that focuses on content, ideas and meaning rather than editing concerns such as sentence structure, paragraphing, spelling. The purpose of the journals is for the students to take time, to think about their process of thinking. Students take many directions. In November, Jerry began a new piece of writing and used the metacognition journal to think about his approach.

> When I was writing, I thought what should I write today? I chose a play. How should I set it up? What are my characters? What is it about? Do I need many people? Do I use large or small things? I think I'm gonna enter it in the Playrush contest. Do I show it to somebody?

Reflection can take several forms. It can be a self-evaluation using stated criteria, like a science-fair project, or the student can use class-generated criteria. In the beginning of each year, we construct as a class an effort chart in an attempt to define exactly what *effort* means. This always creates much discussion (see Fig. 1–5). While the defining terms are often general, the effort chart does provide a beginning vocabulary to assist in self-reflection. We use the chart as a reference point. As the year progresses, the students become more articulate and use the chart less and less. I want the students to realize that effort in trying something new or something hard is a very important part of learning.

New Perceptions

All these activities, such as class meetings and projects and the emphasis on cooperation and trust, have the purpose of building group unity and a learning community. They also model many skills needed in the conference process. The students see they can tackle and succeed in new projects with the encouragement of the group, an idea they will especially rely on when preparing for the first conference. The students recognize that I am not the audience for all they do—there will be a real audience of parents for them at the end of each quarter. Their attitude about learning is positive because of the support of their peers and their self-esteem. When conference time arrives, they are looking forward to sharing their portfolios with their parents. The students have had many opportunities to practice oral skills by sharing ideas, proposing solutions, and expressing opinions. Talking with a group of people is not a new idea to the class. So when the time comes to discuss their work with parents, the idea of sharing is a part of their classroom routine. As the students gain confidence, they assume ownership of their own learning. They become aware of their active role as responsible students. They move from filling the role of a passive student to becoming active members, which is a major shift in their self-perception.

Communication

In addition to developing a new role as active classroom participants, students begin to move toward adopting the role of leader in conference situations. Stepping out of the position of power and offering it to students changed my traditional role as sole informant. I still need to communicate with parents, but now I look for different ways to exchange information. I've discovered that if I want parents to believe and trust their child's information at the conference, I must stay in contact with them on a regular basis. I also think it's important for

Effort Chart

90-100%	I did my <u>very</u> best, tried my hardest, took my time, really concentrated on the task.
80- 89%	I tried hard, but didn't do my very best.
70- 79%	I did what was required, but nothing more
60-69%	I didn't try enough, I didn't think
59% ↓	I didn't think, I rushed and slapped it together

FIGURE 1-5

students, especially sixth graders, to regularly interact with their parents. This is an age when students begin spending more time with peers and parents only receive snatches of information about the child's daily life. I believe that strengthening communication now helps to encourage communication during the teen years.

Parent Letters

The parent letter is a general, all-purpose communication tool (see Fig. 1–6). Sent home every Friday, this is a handwritten information letter written on cherry-pink legal-sized paper. I use the same color paper so the parents will recognize it amid the blizzard of papers they receive. I handwrite it so that it seems more informal and friendly and not so official. The weekly letter keeps the parents informed as to the general activities of the class, and I can address broad issues that concern us all. The letter becomes a window into the class. It also provides a source of discussion between the parent and student, creates a sense of community between families, and provides a forum for my comments.

Take-Home Journal

Another way for me to communicate with parents is the take-home journal. I borrowed this idea from Mary Carolyn Ramsaur, a first-grade teacher at Birch Elementary in Fairbanks, Alaska. Each student has a steno-type notebook for our correspondence. During the week, I write a letter to each parent in this notebook that is personal, not the general informational parent letter on cherry-pink paper. On Friday, the students write a letter to their parents in the same notebook. The students bring the take-home journal home over the weekend so their parents can write in this same notebook short letters to their child and to me (see Figs. 1–7a and 1–7b).

The purpose of the journal is to encourage consistent communication between parent, child, and myself. Most parents use the journal as a place to encourage and reassure their child. I share highlights from the school week, little incidents involving individual children that parents wouldn't normally hear. Along with these generally positive events, I mention any concerns I might have in the journal and ask for advice and assistance from the parent. The take-home journal is also a place to call for a conference if any one of us—parents, child, or me—feels it is necessary.

Since the parents have heard from me on a weekly basis throughout the quarter, there is not much more I could say during an end-of-quarter parent conference. I believe this type of consistent contact

Jan 17

Hi,

Yesterday was National Do Nothing Day. We didn't Celebrate. We've been preparing for parent conferences all week. It looks like everyone has their portfolios ready. Today, We're traveling to University Park Elementary School to be listeners to 3rd graders practice their conferences. Then We'll have another sixth grade class listen while we practice ours. The U. Park sixth graders are learning to do their own parent conferences.

Next week we'll begin a two month focus on Alaska. We'll be looking at the history, people, geography, government, economics, etc. If you have anything you would like to share (pictures, books, experiences, etc), please let me know. This study is a great opportunity for the students to fully understand the uniqueness of Alaska.

We had a very successful emergency bake sale yesterday. The horse riding people called Tuesday and wanted $1200 down payment. Thanks to the bake sale and a

FIGURE 1–6 (continued on page 22)

very generous contribution from a parent, we met the goal. Thank you to all of you who baked and frosted. Next week I'll have information about the upcoming fund raiser. We're still open for ideas.

(Dates to Remember)

Monday, Jan 20th - No school. A teacher workday

Wednesday, Jan 22nd - Student-Parent Conferences from 6:00 p.m. to 7:30 p.m.

Thursday, Jan 23rd - Library walk and lunch at McDonalds. We'll be gone all morning. We're still looking for volunteers.

Friday, January 31st Falcon Festival

We had an Author's Tea on Monday, complete with corsages and raspberry tea. The students shared their books while munching on cookies and homemade scones. Ken made the scones for all of us. He is so thoughtful. I think he sees this class as his too.

I can't believe the warm weather continues.

See you Wednesday.

Kerri

FIGURE 1–6 (continued from page 21)

11-11

Dear Dad,

Halloween was fun but
cold. Do I get to go
trick or treating next year?
When you where little how
much candy did you get?
Can I spend the night at
Bens this weekend? please
I cant wait untill
Cristmas and I know you
got me somthing

love
Daniel

Oct. 31

Hi,

Ken and I moved to Alaska because we both enjoy cold weather. In fact, my favorite temperature is -20°F. Everything is so crisp and clear. Today we made a presentation to our second graders. Daniel created some very interesting sound effects.

Happy Halloween.

Terri

Dear Mrs Austin,

I am glad it's not too cold yet, so the kids can still play outside a lot. But I agree, I like the weather around -20° in the winter. This weekend we made another trip to Fred Meyers, and it seems the choices are overwhelming. Tomorrow my husband and I will fly to Anchorage with Jessie, and I'm looking forward to the trip.

Sincerely

Chris

FIGURE 1–7b

between parent and teacher is necessary if the student-parent conferences are to be successful. Student-led conferences do not mean that the teacher steps totally out of the picture, but they do require the teacher to maintain contact in a different manner. The take-home journal is one way that I share my professional expertise and judgment with the parents.

Building Relationships
The above activities build active and involved relationships between parents, children, and myself. Because the parents and I communicate on a weekly basis, there is time to quickly correct any misunderstanding that might occur. Because we have built a "person" relationship, issues that might be stressful become dialogue points.

I've found that when I share information about my life, students and parents begin to share their lives, too. We begin to see each other as people rather than as the typical "teacher," "parent," or "sixth grader." I am not "her" and the parents are not "they." Together we become an "us." When I talk with parents, I find myself saying that we got a new student or we have an issue to discuss at the next family meeting. I make it a point in weekly parent letters to always mention something about my family or my activities outside of school. It's often said that the more teachers know about students the more effective teachers they become. I also now believe that the more I know and understand the parents, the better teacher I can be for the student. I think that it's also true that the better the parents know me, the more supportive they can be of my teaching. Frank Smith (1986) points out that "Parents should trust teachers—but only if they know what the teachers are doing" (251). I want the parents to know me as a professional and as a person.

While the actual conference portfolio assembly takes about a week, the foundations that support the conference concepts begin on the first day of school and continue throughout the year. The students are ready for student-parent conferences because they are surrounded by an encouraging environment that includes communication and cooperative and supportive people.

Growing in Confidence and Voice 2

Last year, on a cold and snowy January evening, I met with a group of teachers to share ideas about student-parent conferences. After I presented an overview of my process, one teacher, in a very tired voice, asked me if all the work was worth it. I confidently answered, "Yes, of course," and then proceeded to give my reasons why. But while driving home, I thought about that question and my so very confident answer. I definitely could see the benefits of having conferences, but I wondered how my students would answer. So the next morning during our class meeting, I asked them.

MRS. A: Last night, I shared how we do conferences and one teacher asked me if all the work was really worth it. I'd like to know how you feel. Has it made a difference for you? I know it is hard and it takes a lot of time to get everything together, but is it worth it? What do you think?

ANNE: I think it really does make a difference. It's definitely easier because you know the outcome of the conference and you don't get the jitters and all worried wondering about the outcome. It teaches you responsibility while averaging and writing and you also learn while you're getting ready. I admit it is hard but you are also satisfied knowing you can prepare a conference like a teacher can.

DAVE: Yes it does make a difference. It is fun and a new experience. I learned patience and responsibility. I learned to tell the truth and to talk about my grades.

SAMANTHA: I have learned that I could explain myself and my grades. It also teaches me to take my time. I learned that I could do more things if I tried because I thought I never could have done them. I also learned that it is a better way to get in touch with your parents.

PHILIP: I learned I can find trust within my grades and show responsibility as in to make the most of my grades.

MARY: It's scary sometimes.

AARON: It's a very good method.

RICK: I know a lot more about what's going on. Otherwise I don't know what the teacher has said about me. I feel a lot more comfortable doing this. I know my grades and my papers. I seem to know what's going to happen and how I'm doing in school. I'm fair to myself.

DAVID: I learned that I do things that I've never done before and that I can make mistakes sometimes.

MRS. A: Would you recommend this type of conferences to other students and teachers?

[*Everyone agrees they would.*]

MRS. A: What do you think? Should we continue this procedure for the rest of the year?

[*All agree we should.*]

MELISSA: Yes. I think parents understand things better when their child answers their questions. Also, we know the answers to all the questions. Maybe a teacher-parent conference wouldn't answer all their questions.

I was surprised by the strength and conviction of their answers. The students wanted to be in control of the conference situation. They were very aware of their strengths and their weaknesses and seemed comfortable in sharing them with parents. They especially liked the time spent with parents. Participation in the final conference appears to be a strong motivation for all the work involved. I was glad I asked the students; there are many sighs during the preparation time and, if I had used the sighs as a indicator of their enthusiasm, I probably would have quit after the first student-parent conference.

Preparing for the student-parent conference is a great deal of work for me and for the students. After the first conference, however, it is much easier and the students can do much of the preparation without my direct instruction. Students become very proficient in self-assessing and in assembling all the parts needed for student-parent conferences. During the morning meeting discussion, Mary had said that conferences can be scary. Mary was a new student who happened to arrive on the tail end of conference preparation and was feeling overwhelmed. I do, however, agree with her statement. Without adequate preparation, a student can feel lost and unprepared for a potentially stressful situation. Preparation is the key as each stage builds upon another. In each step, the student is required to gather information and then consider how that information reflects on them as a learner. Preparation involves:

- identifying common values, particularly concrete characteristics of a "good student"
- assembling the components of the conference portfolio by gathering information about themselves as learners
- a teacher-student conference discussing the results of the gathered data and completing the report card
- a student practice conference verbally rehearsing the conference

Each step prepares the student for the next step. Beginning with identifying common values sets the stage for the other types of preparation that follow.

Identifying Common Values

Steve Covey states in the *Seven Habits of Highly Effective People* that an effective goal "identifies where you want to be, helps determine where you are, gives important information on how to get there, and tells you when you've arrived" (137). This is exactly what finding and identifying common values does—it sets the direction for the year. I discussed this concept with Terry Johnson, who suggested that I somehow mesh the community and the classroom values to build a stronger, more unified view of assessment. I needed to find out what parents valued. Intellectually, I knew this was an important direction to take. I was, however, very nervous about asking parents what they value for their child in our classroom. I knew what I wanted and, frankly, I didn't want them to interfere with "my program." What if they valued the ten comprehension questions at the end each of each chapter? or daily worksheets? If I knew what they valued, then I would have to deal with it in some way. With the encouragement of Shirley Kaltenbach, a third-grade teacher and my research colleague, I did ask and was surprised with what I found.

Before I asked the parents, however, I wanted to be clear about my own values, so I compiled a list.

- the willingness to try something new, to take risks, and to know
  that mistakes are OK
- the willingness to help others, to cooperate, and to compromise
- responsibility for personal actions
- honesty with me, and with other students
- a love of learning

After I composed my list, I was ready to find out what the classroom community—kids, parents, and myself—valued. Since most of my parents attend our open house, it seemed like the perfect time to ask the parents.

Open House Survey

During the open house held the first week of school, I asked parents to imagine their child six years from now, when the child has just completed twelve years of schooling. How will that child be? Not what will they be, but how will they be? When I asked this question last year, the parents got very quiet. Finally one father tentatively raised his hand and asked, "Does spelling count?" This broke the tension, we all laughed, and—after I explained the idea of a fast-write—they all busily began writing. Sue wrote about her son, Aaron.

> I expect my child to be ready to challenge his future, to be unsure of his direction, maybe knowing more what he doesn't want than what he does want. To be confident and excited about getting on with life. To want to stretch his wings and want to let go—but still knowing he can fall back to a place of safety.

Another parent wrote,

> I expect Rose will be the kind of person that I not only love, but like, respect, and admire. I expect that as she matures to graduation she will not only know right from wrong, but always try to do what is right. I expect that Rose will have consideration for others and identify her goals and interests and I'll support her in whatever she chooses to do.

Laurie said,

> My son Gary is a super-kid. He's confident, calm, and wise. His face is shining—he's so excited to be graduating. His grade point average isn't 4.0 [As]—but that's OK; he's

learned much in his 12 years of school! He's learned how
to be independent, kind to others, helpful, and creative.
He's not afraid to take risks. I am very proud of him because
I know whatever road he chooses in life (whatever profes-
sion)—he'll be just *fine!*

I was very eager to read all the responses. Surprisingly, I've found
the parents to be concerned with the total child rather than specific skill
mastery. The parent information fell into two groups: social and academic.

Academic
learned how to study
go to college
graduate with honors
knowledgeable about all subjects
solid learning foundation

Social
confident
calm
independent
kind to others
helpful
creative
not afraid to take risks
mature
caring
respond responsively to world situations
self-assured
gives best effort
do what is right

In the social category, I included all the comments regarding
characteristics such as confidence, kindness, and creativity. I placed any
specific reference to school, grades, or subjects in the academic list.
Academic comments tended to be very general such as to graduate with
honors or to be knowledgeable about all the school-covered subjects.
I was surprised that the parents weren't more specific in this area. No
parent said they wanted their child to read in the ninety-ninth percentile
or be a whiz in fractions. The results of the parent responses and my
list became the topic for a class discussion the next day. This led us to
the next step in discovering our class values.

Good Student vs. Good Grades

During the class discussion of the parent responses the next day, the students puzzled over the concept of a "good student." The class thought their parents wanted them to get good grades, so they were surprised when this wasn't the focus of their parents' comments. This led us to a discussion about whether it is better to be a good student or be a student that gets good grades. This always generates lots of talk, so I suggested that we find out what our community thinks about that question. The students interviewed parents, other teachers, and their peers. In one interview, a parent stated, "I'd like you to be a good student, because being a good student can get good grades too. When you're a good student learning comes easier." Another student noted the following after an interview:

> My mom said she would rather have me be a good student. My mom said a good student usually has a better attitude about life, socializing, and a broader outlook. School is not the end all or be all of life. Also that grades are not a measurement of success, but a tool used to measure knowledge. That being the best you can be in all things is a better measurement of success. That's what my mom would have me be.

Teachers respond in a similar manner. The reading teacher stated, "To be a good student, because it's a lifelong attitude, unlike good grades, which only last one year." All parents and teachers said that being a good student was more important than being a student with good grades.

The term *good student* has no meaning to most of my students before we explore its limits. They know they should be a good student, but many don't have a clue about how to go about being one. Vygotsky (1978) notes that a word without meaning is an empty sound (120), and, during an oral presentation in 1990, Terry Johnson suggested that teachers have a concrete picture of a successful student. With these two thoughts in mind, the students and I set out to define and identify concrete, observable traits of a "good student."

Student Panel Discussion

We decided the best way to find out about being a good student was to ask one. The class identified six "good" students in the school and invited them to participate in a panel discussion during lunch. As everyone ate, we asked questions (the panel members are simply identified by *student* and a number).

DALE: How do you get smart?

STUDENT 1: Study.

STUDENT 2: Work hard.

STUDENT 4: I study every night.

AARON: Do you do homework right away?

STUDENT 3: Yeah, as soon as I get home.

AARON: If you're not good in a subject, do you get good grades in it?

STUDENT 1: Kind of.

STUDENT 3: Yeah.

STUDENT 2: Most of the time.

ROSE: How do you get to be a good student?

STUDENT 3: I just work hard and turn all my work in.

JAKE: Are your assignments always turned in on time?

STUDENT 1: Yes.

[*The rest of the panel nods in agreement.*]

AARON: Do you guys have any lucky charms or something like that I can borrow?

[*The panel laughs and all of them shake their heads.*]

AARON: Do you get good grades for yourself or your parents?

STUDENT 3: Myself, mostly.

SHIRLEY: Why do you get good grades? Do you get paid or get in trouble if you don't?

STUDENT 1: I just want to. For me.

AARON: Is your schoolwork always first? What comes first, schoolwork or like, say, sports? Say you have a basketball game or something you really like. Do you stay home and do homework or go to the game?

STUDENT 5: Do homework.

STUDENT 3: I'd stay and do homework.

STUDENT 4: I'd stay home.

STUDENT 1: I'd stay.

STUDENT 2: I'd stay and go to the game when I finish.

JAKE: Do you have a certain place to do homework?

STUDENT 4: In my room.

STUDENT 3: At my desk in my room.

SUE: Do you think of yourself as a good student?

STUDENT 4: Sometimes.

[*The rest of the panel nods.*]

AARON: How do you get to be a good student? What is the key to
success?

STUDENT 5: Study hard, study everything. Study for one hour every
night.

STUDENT 4: Work at it.

STUDENT 3: Don't give up. Don't have your parents do all your work.
Take responsibility.

STUDENT 2: Turn everything in. Get homework in on time.

STUDENT 1: Listen to the teacher, follow directions.

After lunch and our guests left, we discussed what surprised us
about the panel responses. Ken said, "I was surprised that they all did
their homework when they got home right away," an opinion repeated
by many of my students. Nick made another common comment, stating,
"I was surprised at the things they said about doing their homework
first, instead of going to the game." For some of my students, this was
the first time they had considered effort to be a part of obtaining good
grades. Another common reaction was the idea of making good grades
for oneself and not to please someone else, which led to a discussion
about learning being a personal goal and not something that parents
made you do.

We took this information, combined it with the data from the
parent and teacher interviews, and attempted to make sense of it all by
trying to identify patterns or repeating themes. Last year, we decided
that effort and responsibility were traits that parents and other teachers
valued, and they seemed to be common characteristics of the identified
"good" students. Effort and responsibility then became our two goals
for the year.

Concept Circles

We now knew what was important to us, but students needed a concrete
picture of effort and responsibility, so we spent one morning defining
each term. I used the idea of concept circles, which I borrowed from the
Equals math program (1990). The concept circle is a graphic organizer
consisting of three concentric circles. The global term is placed in the
center. Next, the students use the middle circle to list three or four
words that define the global term. Then the students carefully examine
each of the words in the middle circle, using very definite and concrete
terms to define each of the words. In essence, as the circles grow larger,

the terms become more specific. This process of definition provides the students with vocabulary and concrete ways to reach the global term in the center of the circle (see Figs. 2–1a and 2–1b). I put these circles up on the wall so that students can refer to them. These words become part of the class vocabulary. We use them in class discussions, when constructing personal goals, and in reflective writing.

Periodically throughout the quarter, I ask the students to reflect on their effort and responsibility at home and at school. During the first quarter, Samantha used these terms to specifically examine her actions.

> Responsibility at school—I have trust in people. You can't have belief, trust, count on someone or they can't count on you to be a responsible friend or person. I treat other people's property as if it was my own . . . I always leave it in good shape. I wouldn't leave it in bad shape and then they won't let me use it anymore. My desk is always ready for Mrs. A. to look at . . . I write down my work because I don't want to forget it. I double check my work to see if I have everything I need.
>
> Responsibility at home—I know my family can count on me. I keep my stuff at home neat, clean, and I make sure that everything I need for the next day is ready.
>
> Effort at school . . . I follow directions to things and I listen to directions for something too. I take risks by guessing answers to things. I try new things like I find a new way to do my homework that is hard, when I am at school I ask the teacher for help on something. I just don't give up on things. I believe in myself. I believe in myself that I could do something that I never tried before. I believe in others. Like I believe that they could do whatever. I also think to get the job done. Like I sit there and think up and answer that I know and I take my time thinking of a good way to answer things. . . . I share my work with others by sharing my opinions and answers of things to others. I also consider other's opinions like I listen to other people's opinions and agree with them it is an opinion that I can understand. I listen to theirs by listening to their problems, questions, etc. But I don't ignore them.
>
> Effort at home—At home: I take risks at home like in

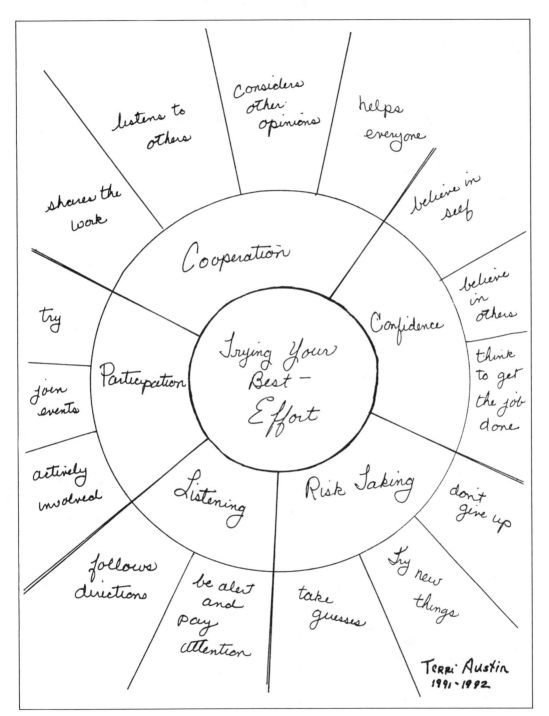

FIGURE 2–1a

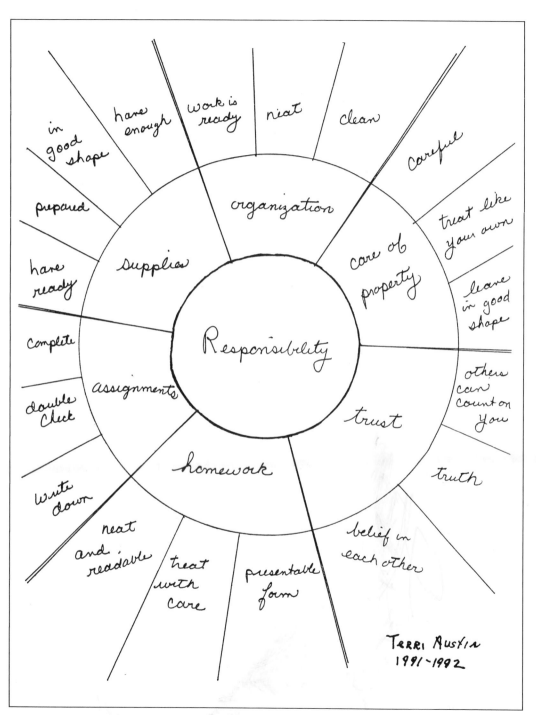

FIGURE 2–1b

cooking, I guess a lot of stuff for measuring. I also try new
things to add to my cooking. And I don't give up on cooking. I keep on cooking. . . . I always have belief in myself
for when I am babysitting. I always get the job done when
I am babysitting. I help my sisters and parents learn at home.
I share my thoughts and stuff with them. I listen to my
sisters when they talk to me. I share my work or what I
learned from my work to my family.

Samantha has learned a lot about herself by participating in the reflective
process. She's beginning to critically examine herself by the standards
that our community values. She's connecting home and school, reinforc-
ing the idea that learning happens everywhere.

The strongest part of this identification process is the communication that develops between the parents, students, and myself. Together
we have discussed and shared what we think is important and attempted
to put nebulous terms into specific words. Rexford Brown in *Schools
of Thought* says, "As soon as people begin to focus on their language,
a literacy of thoughtfulness has gained a toehold, and community building has begun" (1991, 235). This process binds us together into a
community with a shared vocabulary. We can now talk about a successful student in terms that we all understand and accept. The concreteness
of these terms makes them attainable and we are all heading in the same
direction with the same purpose (Covey 1989).

Portfolios

Once we have a common vision and vocabulary, the students begin to
collect and assemble information about themselves as learners. We save
all written work (what I call pencil-and-paper work) in a classroom
portfolio. I take a picture of anything that won't fit into the classroom
portfolio such as science projects or large artwork. We save everything in
preparation for the student-parent conferences. All through the quarter,
students practice reflective thinking. After completing an assignment,
I often ask students to reflect on the task using the values we identified
as important (see Fig. 2–2). "Using the terms on the wall, how did
you do?"

As they move through this process, students gain the ability to
step back out of themselves and think critically in relation to what they
have learned and how they attempted the task (Harp 1991). This ability
to reflect is vital for the students if they are to accurately examine
themselves as learners when assembling their conference portfolios.

Jan. 21

My grade for effort and responsibility would probably be a 99% because I was very resposible in mixing and measuring the dough. I was also responsible to clean the dishes we used and cleaning up our working area.

FIGURE 2–2

Conference Portfolios

The purpose of the conference portfolio is to gather items that present a total picture of the student as a learner. As a teacher, I've always had the forum to express my opinion about students, but the conference portfolio offers an opportunity for students, parents, and other teachers to share their insights as well. These opinions and insights are viewed as equally important as my comments. Because this portfolio is a reflection of the student as a total learner, it contains elements that build on that purpose. The contents change somewhat each year as each class is a bit different. Last year the conference portfolios contained:

- two papers from each subject area with student justification
- one page photocopied from two books read during the quarter
- one photocopied journal page
- one piece of writing
- grade graphs for each subject
- a parent comment sheet
- the classroom teacher's (me) narrative
- another teacher's comment sheet
- a summary sheet
- student grade reflections
- a report card
- the goals for the following quarter

In *Schools of Thought,* Brown states,

> If you want to change individuals, you usually have to make them conscious of things that are right in front of their faces, things that they cannot see while everyone else can. You often have to help them learn how to listen to themselves, how to recognize contradictions in what they are saying. (1991, 234)

Another purpose of the portfolio contents is to create a situation in which students must examine their own learning. Do their actions fit their intentions? In the past, it's been too easy for my students to blame poor grades on external influences such as teachers, sickness, parents, or sports. When students are required to gather information and then reflect on the meaning of that information, they are put in a position of assuming responsibility for their actions. In *Expanding Student Assessment,* Perrone states,

> The most important assessment takes place on a smaller and even more informal level. . . . [Assessment] takes place in

the individual student who is constantly assessing her own work, deciding what is right and wrong, what fits and what does not, what is a "good enough" job. This self-appraisal is the ultimate focus of all standards. (1991, 37)

I want students to truthfully know themselves as they are and not use excuses. When students know their strengths and weaknesses, they are capable of making changes in their learning habits. The first time students compile a conference portfolio, they often are surprised by their discoveries about themselves. This discovery process begins when students self-select papers. Through the course of the quarter, for instance, Allysa would often blame others for not having her work. "I turned it in, you lost it" or "I had it on my desk, someone took it" were daily comments. After completing the first quarter conference portfolio where she had to honestly examine all her work, Allysa commented, "I guess I need to turn in all my work. I don't have much to look at." This was the first time that Allysa connected her personal responsibility of completing and turning in her work to herself. This was a major realization for her.

Self-Selected Papers and Reflection
Students are required to choose two papers from each subject area. Each paper must reflect the student as a learner in some way. Since each chosen paper must be accompanied by the reason it was picked, the student must be clear as to the purpose for choosing the paper. Saying "I picked this paper because I got a good grade on it" is not appropriate. The student needs to be more specific. As a beginning, I model responses on the board and we discuss them together. I usually outlaw the use of "worked hard" and "tried hard." The students need to be more specific and concisely address what they learned from the work. Surprisingly, most students don't pick their papers with the highest scores. It's hard to talk about what they learned from a paper that received a 100 percent. Ruth chose a social studies paper about latitude and longitude. She earned a 34 percent on the assignment. When I asked her why she chose that particular paper, she explained, "I didn't know how to do it then, but I can do it now." She then showed me that she could use latitude and longitude to identify locations. Gary chose two very different assignments in social studies. The first was a test on naming the countries in the Middle East on which he received a 63 percent. The second was a scrapbook on the Yukon Quest, a dog-sled race between Whitehorse, Canada, and Fairbanks, Alaska (see Fig.

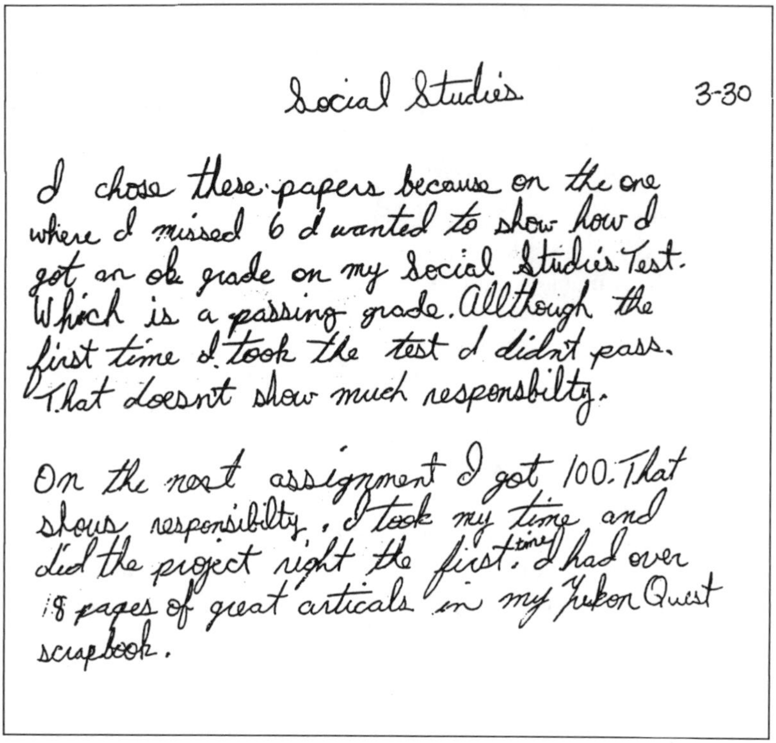

Social Studies   3-30

I chose these papers because on the one
where I missed 6 I wanted to show how I
got an ok grade on my Social Studies Test.
Which is a passing grade. Allthough the
first time I took the test I didn't pass.
That doesn't show much responsbilty.

On the next assignment I got 100. That
shows responsibilty. I took my time and
did the project right the first time. I had over
18 pages of great articals in my Yukon Quest
scrapbook.

FIGURE 2–3

2–3). In his reflections, Gary writes that he didn't show much responsibility on the map test and received only a passing grade. He then describes his work on the scrapbook assignment. Gary's reflections show his growing awareness that his specific efforts can affect his learning.

The act of self-reflecting begins the shift of each student into an active role of assessment and away from a role of passivity (Perrone 1991). Through the physical and mental act of writing about how that particular paper represents them as a learner, the students will grapple with finding accurate, descriptive vocabulary. They can begin to paint real pictures of themselves as learners and then begin to assume responsibility for their own learning. This process also shows students that I value the process of learning rather than the product (Routman 1991).

Book Selection
The next entry into the conference portfolio is a representation of each student's reading for the quarter. If we're reading a class novel, I photocopy a page for everyone to include. Each student also chooses

any two books they read during the quarter and photocopies one page from each book. Again, the student must say why they choose that particular book to include in the conference portfolio. Jerome chose *Where The Red Fern Grows.* He wrote,

> I picked this book cause I can relate to it in many ways. I always had a hunger in my heart for my very own dog. I have a particular breed, it's German Shepherd. My grandma said when I come back I can get one. I can't wait.

Students are again practicing self-reflection, although this time it is focused on reading choices. This reflection also gives information about reading ability and reading interests.

Personal Journals

Following the same pattern as the reading books, students choose one page from their personal journal written during the quarter to give a picture of their daily informal writing (see Fig. 2–4).

Best Piece of Writing

Students choose their best piece of writing for the quarter and most select a published piece. This means that the writing has gone through many draft and revision stages and has been edited by peers. After the final editing, students can publish it in any form, such as a book, poster, letter, etc. The second quarter, Samantha chose her published book titled *A Christmas Surprise.* It's a romantic story written in five chapters. Her reflections include the specifics of editing and publishing the book and the problems she encountered.

> My book has a neatly colored cover, insides and illustrations. I also made my handwriting neat. Also it was neatly put together. I took my time on making it. I spelled all the words correctly in pen.
>
> In my writing I had problems in my last chapter, because I had to add some more sentences and write it over to get my book interesting enough for people to like it. I also had a problem in how am I going to make my book, how am I going to write it, but I figured it out. I put effort and time to come to school adding stuff.

Grade Graphs

The next element in the portfolio is the grade graphs. I've discovered that students need a way to visually see their recorded grades. It's

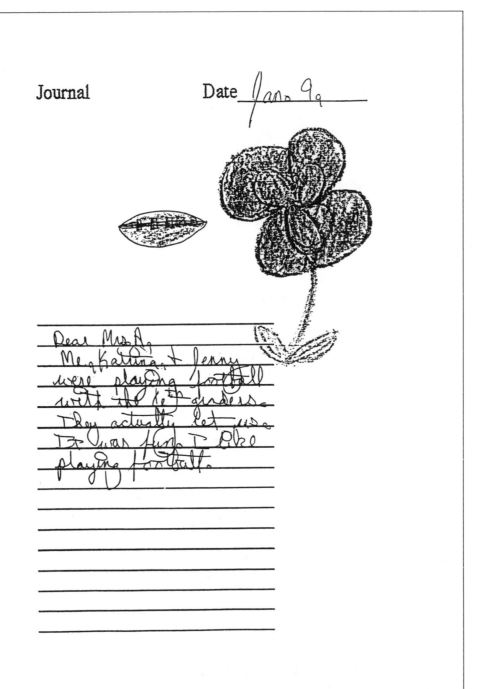

Journal   Date _Jan. 9q_

Dear Mrs. A,
Me, Katrina, + Jenny
were playing football
with the 1st graders.
They actually let us.
It was fun. I like
playing football.

FIGURE 2–4

common to want to remember only the best, and many students remember the good scores while they tend to forget the not-so-good scores. Grade graphs have helped to solve this problem. Using graph paper, each student creates a blank graph for each subject. Along the vertical axis, each student numbers from zero to one hundred by fives. Using a light-colored pencil, the students shade in the spaces from seventy to seventy-nine, creating a colored bar across the C range on the graph, which is a visual picture of average scores. Many students believe that eighty to eighty-nine is average, and I want them to be aware that As and Bs require extra effort.

After the student creates a bar graph for each subject (see Fig. 2–5), I individually meet with each student and read off the recorded grades for every subject. After the graphs are completed, the student averages each subject three times. When a student arrives at the same answer three times, he goes to a partner and the partner also averages the grades. The partner's answer must agree. If not, they both average again. The students become very adept and accurate at averaging. When completed, the graph is a very strong visual picture of the grades for each student. Students can also examine each subject in relation to the other. They can see whether they need to put more effort into one subject by comparing the visual representation of the graphs. Trends can be noted. Are tests consistently low? Are long-term projects consistently high? These observations and reflections are one piece of information that can help students set goals for the next quarter.

All of the information so far has been self-selected and/or compiled by the student. They've chosen papers from each subject, a page from two books, a journal page, a piece of writing, and grade graphs from each subject. Additional information is needed to have a well-rounded picture of the student, so we look to parents, other adults, and me, the classroom teacher.

Parent Comment Sheets

The students ask their parents to complete an open-ended comment sheet to be included in the conference portfolio. When I first tried this, I developed a checklist, thinking it would be easier and more parents would complete it. Although it seemed to work, I quickly abandoned it. I realized I was still controlling the responses because of the limited choices presented to the parents. Now it is very open ended and parents can take it in any direction they wish (see Fig. 2–6).

Karen Mitchell, a third-grade teacher at Harborview Elementary in Juneau, Alaska, takes this one step further. She asks parents to write

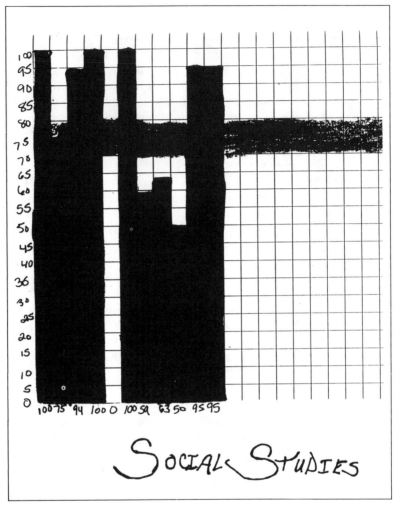

FIGURE 2–5

an open letter to their child concerning their views of the child as a learner, as a friend, and as a person in general. In a personal interview I had with her, Karen stated, "I spent a lot time crying while reading these heartfelt, well thought out letters." The parent comment sheets provide an opportunity four times a year for parents to share their observations, thoughts, and feelings with their child.

The actual form changes as the year progresses. During the first quarter the form looks like the one in Fig. 2–6. Because the year is

Dear _____,

    I am beginning to prepare for our Student/Parent conference. I need your help. Please complete the following statements. These are your observations of me at home; it doesn't need to be long. I need this sheet returned by Monday, so that I can incorporate the information in our conference.

                      Thank you,

                    _____

My thoughts about _____ as a reader at home,

_____
_____
_____
_____
_____
_____

My thoughts about _____ as a writer at home,

_____
_____
_____
_____
_____

My thoughts about _____ as a mathematician and scientist at home,

_____
_____
_____
_____
_____

Other comments and observations about _____ as a learner at home. (You may want to consider effort, responsibility, and risk taking)

_____
_____
_____
_____
_____

Parent observation sheet – Terri Austin

FIGURE 2–6

half over at the end of the second quarter, the form asks for any observed changes (see Fig. 2–7). The third-quarter form is the same as the first quarter's, and the end-of-the-year form (the fourth quarter) is very open ended. It asks for parents to review growth and changes over the whole year. On the last comment sheet of the year, Jason's parents wrote,

> The transformation of Jason as a student has been remarkable, from an F and C− student to an A and B student. We cannot help but believe that a great deal of the credit must go to the manner in which class materials are presented and the curriculum is organized. Jason certainly has become more focused upon his capabilities rather than his limitations. The general emphasis upon responsibility for one's own actions and performance has also been most beneficial. Jason was a very frustrated young man in Germany and has had a tendency to place blame on others rather than accepting responsibility for his own choices. The last portion of this year has wrought welcome changes in this respect. Though not always the most conscientious student, he puts forth serious effort on his studies and assumes responsibility for the results of his effort. We believe that the "writing classroom" environment has been crucial to Jason's educational development, self-examination, and personal growth.

In the beginning I was concerned with whether or not parents would be willing to complete the form. I've found the majority of parents happy to do so. They do need plenty of time, however, so the comment sheet goes home about a week before it's actually needed. For those parents who speak or write little English, the student interviews his parents and writes the responses. Occasionally, a parent will refuse to participate. When this happens, I ask the student if they want me to intervene. The student knows their home better than I do, of course, and sometimes it is best if I don't pursue this issue. When it does happen, the student and I look for a substitute "parent." This could be a Boy Scout or youth group leader, a coach, another teacher in the building, or any other significant adult in the child's life. I feel the information on this sheet contains information that is important for the student in the evaluation process, so the student and I work to solve obstacles. In the past four years, I've only twice had to find an alternate adult.

There are three major purposes for the parental comment sheet. First, several years ago I read Taylor and Dorsey-Gaines' *Growing Up*

Dear _____,

      I am beginning to prepare for our second Student/Parent Conference. Again, I need your views about me as a learner at home. The school year is half over. Please think about me and how I've changed since the beginning of the year. I need this sheet by Tuesday, so that I can incorporate the information in our conference.

                      Thank you,

Changes I've noticed in _____ as a reader at home,
_____
_____
_____
_____
_____

Changes I've noticed in _____ as a writer at home,
_____
_____
_____
_____

Changes I've noticed in _____ as a mathematician and scientist at home,
_____
_____
_____
_____

Changes I've noticed in _____ in effort and responsibility at home,
_____
_____
_____
_____

Parent observation sheet – Terri Austin

FIGURE 2–7

Literate (1988), and I was astonished at the amount of learning that happens at home. Somehow it never occurred to me that this kind of learning should be tied into school. I finished the book determined to find a way to include home knowledge in assessment. Second, I realized that parents were an untapped source of information about my students. They see my students in many situations that I never will. Third, I hoped that by completing the comment sheet, parents might look at their child a little differently. Seeing daily activities in the light of learning situations might change their perceptions of their child. Fourth, as Weaver says, when parents are invited to tell their own stories about their children, both parent and teacher become better observers of those children (1988). If we share our knowledge, we all benefit. Fifth, I hoped students would see that learning happens everywhere in their lives, not just in school. I really wanted students to know what their parents thought, to see themselves through the eyes of their parents. I've found the parent comment form a way to serve all these purposes.

Another Teacher's Comment Sheet
This is similar in form and purpose to the parent's comment sheet. I wanted to give other teachers a place to share their observations and comments about the learner. When I tentatively presented the idea to my staff, I didn't know how they would feel about the extra work, but they all agreed to give it a try. The reading teacher said that she was excited to finally find a place where she could say something that was valued (see Fig. 2–8). Two years later, they are still completing the comment forms for students.

To keep it from becoming a burden for everyone, there are a few rules I ask the students to follow. First, a student must approach and ask the staff member to complete the form. The teacher has every right to say no with no guilt attached. Second, any adult in the building that has contact with the student can be asked, even though the form specifically refers to teachers. The janitor, the librarian, and the bilingual aide are all good candidates. Third, the form must be presented a week before it's due. The student can't wait till the last minute. Fourth, the student has to ask a different teacher each quarter; they can't continually use the librarian or the basketball coach. The student personally collects the comment sheet and stores it in the conference portfolio.

Karen Mitchell approaches the comment sheet a little differently for her classes. Her students make their own appointments with other

Dear *Mrs. Eliot*

    This week I am preparing for my Student-Parent conference. To help me prepare for this, would you please fill out the following form. Please consider each section carefully and be honest. I need this sheet returned by *Thursday*, so that I can incorporate the information in my conference.

                                      Thank you,

                                        Mary

1. *Mary* as a group or team member. (This includes sharing the work, listening to others, considering other's opinions, and helping others learn)
Gary's listening skills are improving.

2. *Mary* as a risk taker. (This includes taking guesses, trying new things, and not giving up.)
Gary seems to be willing to try new things– even dance!!! He just needs a little encouragement

3. *Mary* as showing effort. (This includes participation, listening, risk taking, cooperation.)
Gary's listening skills are improving as is his participation.

4. *Mary* as a responsible learner. (This includes being trustworthy, turning in assignments, taking care of property and being organized.)
Gary treats instruments properly.

Additional teacher reflection form - Terri Austin

FIGURE 2–8

teachers and then report back to Karen, who constructs a master schedule. Karen states,

> They [the students] were responsible for keeping the appointments and only two were missed, which were later rescheduled. It was interesting to see which teachers the children chose, especially from the knowledge of what they were being evaluated. Often the non-risk-takers chose teachers whom they knew would be easier on them. A few chose the person they knew would be the most honest. That, in itself, was a real risk.

My Narrative

Another element in the conference portfolio is my narrative. While the parents and teachers are completing their comment sheets, I'm writing personal narratives for each student. I used to sit down at my computer and spend all weekend writing the twenty-eight narratives. A couple of years later and a bit wiser, I've figured out a way to make the task easier.

1. I've learned to take daily observational notes. At first I tried writing on sticky notes, but they soon lost their stickiness and became trails of little yellow papers. Now I use computer address labels, the kind that come thirty on page. I carry a clipboard with me and a page of the labels.
2. I only focus on six to seven students a day. I used to try and watch every student every day. I discovered that I only observed those students who demanded my attention and I never wrote anything about the students who were quiet. I also never purposefully observe students on Friday. I'm tired and we have the most interruptions on that day. Of course, if something significant happens on any day, I record that, but I try to focus on a limited number of students each day.
3. Each student has a page in a large notebook. At the end of each day, I insert the label on the student's page. This provides me with a permanent record. Each label contains the name of the student, the date, and the subject or topic during the observation (see Fig. 2–9). This page then becomes the basis for my quarterly narratives. Some teachers use only grades while others use a combination of grades, anecdotal records, behavior charts, and so on.
4. I write six to seven narratives at a time to spread out the task. The writing remains fresh and I don't end up exhausted. One time I tried

Anne 1-21
Responsibility - reading
silently after break

Anne 1-21
did a lot of cleaning
after baking

Anne
reading quietly

Anne 1-21
reading after copying
overhead math

Anne 1-21
baking - organized and
follows directions

Anne 1-24
just to finish reading
and writing of s.s.

Anne 1-28
working well, cooperating
with dawn

Anne 1-30
Comp. Lab - willing to
take risks

Anne 2-4
s.s. taking notes from
lecture

Anne 2-4
Responsibility - reading
when journal is
finished

Anne 2-4
Writing - copy over story -
revising?

Anne 2-6
Drew map & maze at home
for mystery story. Will be
part of her book

Anne 2-12
Organizing valentine
making group

Anne 2-12
Writing - O.L & P. with
small group

Anne 2-12
Status of class -
reading

Anne 2-12
Cleaning up more than
others in group

Anne 2-12
helping to monitor
loudness of open group

Reading - 2-25
recorder of group
super cooperation
constructing grids

FIGURE 2-9

writing the narratives during class while the students worked on their portfolios. It didn't work at all for me as I couldn't concentrate on the writing. Now I do the narratives during the evening at home.

5. I address the narratives to the child. Since the child is the primary audience, it makes sense to do this, and I've found that it's easier to write the narrative (see Fig. 2–10). The completed narrative then becomes part of the conference portfolio and the student will use this information on the summary sheet.

The Summary Sheet

The student now has a great deal of information. They have their own reflections, their grade graphs, examples of reading and writing, and comments from parents, another teacher, and me. To help them organize and synthesize all the data, they complete the summary sheet (see Fig. 2–11).

The summary sheet is a large spreadsheet that contains all the gathered comments. In the first column, students review all their fast-writes, reading and writing samples, and grades. After this review, they write in their comments. I've found that it's important for the students to complete this column first. If they do the others first, they tend to repeat what I say or what their parents say. The next column is for parental comments. The students are to read and paraphrase the parent's written statements; the paraphrasing itself is important as it requires the student to understand the comments. The student then does the same for the rest of the summary sheet. When the summary sheet is completed, it provides a total picture of the students as learners from their own view, their parent's perspective, their classroom teacher's (my) opinion, and another adult's position.

Grade Reflections

With all this information in mind, each student begins to formulate grades. Since grades are required in my district, the students and I decide how we will arrive at the final grades for the report card. Last year, we decided to count the paper-and-pencil grade averages (the grade graphs) as 50 percent of the total grade and the two class values of effort and responsibility as the remaining 50 percent. The graph grades are already averaged, but at this stage, the students need an effort and responsibility grade for each subject area. To determine one grade for both effort and responsibility in each subject, students refer to our established values and the definitions posted on the wall and to the portfolio items chosen for that particular subject. With all these in

October 17

Dear Sarah,

The beginning of the year is a time to get to know each other, find out what you know and find the best way that I can aid your learning. For that reason, I've done lots of watching. The thing that struck me most about you is that you are a reader. You read every single minute you aren't doing something else. Today I watched you read during lunch. You were so intent in the story, you hardly noticed what you were eating. You also smoothly read out loud with much expression. You read many kinds of materials, from fairy tales, picture books to long novels like <u>Maniac McGee</u>. Your writing reflects your reading ability. Your text flows smoothly from one idea to the next. Tied into all of this are your art ideas. The pictures from <u>Peppermint in the Parlor</u> and <u>Princess Bride</u> show that you can listen and create pictures from what you hear.

I love it when you share your ideas in class. You always add much to the discussion. You are a strong performer. During our musical performance last week, you knew all your lines and followed stage directions well. I could tell that you have been in front of an audience before. You had the same quality of work when you were one of the presidential candidates. You knew your platform and your issues.

Your work shows that you are a disciplined student. You always know your poem and it's evident that you studied for the several tests we've had. You think through problems. An example of this is gathering and organizing data and creating a highly readable graph. I know that along with breaking some school records, you go to gymnastics three times a week.

You are a good strong student. I'm really proud of all that you have learned this quarter.

Love,

M. A

FIGURE 2–10

Name _____

Date _____

Grade _____

Learning Area	Student Reflection	Teacher Reflection	Parent Reflection	Other Adult Reflection
Effort, Responsibility				
Language Arts: Reading				
Language Arts: Writing				
Math				
Science				
Social Studies				

Student Summary--Terri Austin

FIGURE 2–11

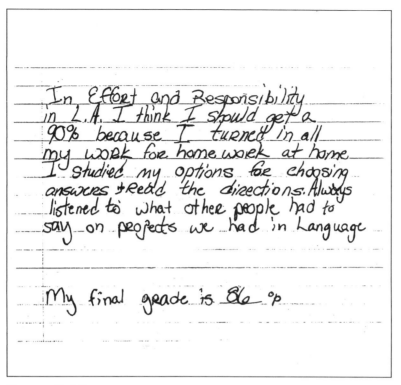

In Effort and Responsibility
in L.A. I think I should get a
90% because I turned in all
my work for home work at home.
I studied my options for choosing
answers + Read the directions. Always
listened to what other people had to
say on projects we had in Language

My final grade is 86 %

FIGURE 2–12

mind, students do a fast write for each subject, arriving at a grade reinforced with reasons, examples, and justifications (see Fig. 2–12). They then take the grade graph grade and the effort and responsibility grade and average them together for a final grade in each subject. This method allows students who aren't good at paper-and-pencil tasks to count effort and responsibility (our class values) as equally valuable. Each year the class and I reach this method of calculating grades after a lengthy discussion. We all share experiences where we tried our best but still didn't do well on homework, tests, and other activities. Every class feels that our class values should count for something and each year the class comes to the same conclusion. After our discussion, it always turns out that the paper and pencil items should count for 50 percent and our values should count for 50 percent.

With all this information neatly organized and summarized in the conference portfolio, the student is ready for an individual conference with me.

Student-Teacher Conferences

The students sign up on the chalkboard when they are ready to conference with me. They bring their completed portfolio and together we review the contents. I ask that each student review everything: all the papers and fast-writes; the journal page; the piece of writing; the comments from parents, me, and another adult; the summary sheet; and the grade reflections.

The student-teacher conferences provide an initial practice of presenting the sum of information. I'm also seeing the total portfolio for the first time. I look for completion of tasks and consistency in conclusions. For example, a student can't give himself a 98 percent in effort and responsibility if he's missing thirteen out of twenty assignments in math. All statements must be backed up by observable facts.

After reviewing the portfolio, we discuss grades for the report card. Ninety-nine percent of the time, the student gives himself a grade very close to what I had in mind. If we agree, then the student fills out the report card while I watch. This step is important—very important. Having the student complete the report card continues to build ownership in this entire process. The grades belong to the student and, at this point, the student should understand completely the reason for each grade.

If we don't agree, we talk. In the first quarter, I usually find there are three types of students that arrive at misplaced grades. The first group consists of the overachievers, and they are usually girls. They can't bring themselves to give themselves appropriately high marks. A typical response is, "I deserve a B- in math, because I didn't try hard enough and I could have done better." When this occurs we review their portfolio, and I point out all their growth and accomplishments. Then I ask them to go back, think about it, and then review their grades. When they return for a second conference, their grades usually more accurately reflect their learning. After the first quarter, this group rarely has problems again. They seem to understand it's all right to give yourself a high grade if you deserve it. Other teachers have found the same thing and, again, it happens mostly with females.

The second group consists of students who think they can manipulate the system to get good grades. Because they must show proof of every statement, this attitude doesn't last long. As a professional, I have the right to disagree with their conclusions, and I do if they aren't accurately looking at all the data. After we review their portfolio together, they return to their seat to rethink and rewrite their grade reflections. We do this as many times as it requires for the student to accept an accurate picture of themselves as a learner. This group also usually only has problems during the first quarter. After that, the student has a better grasp of what is expected and what is acceptable.

The last group of students includes those who only examine one part of the portfolio to determine their final grade. These students typically cling to the grade graphs. Numbers have a strong power and seem more legitimate and real. As I conference with them, I take extra time to go over the other elements of the portfolio. I stress that the grade graphs are just *one* part of a total picture. In the majority of cases, by the second quarter they begin to expand their views of themselves as learners.

One time, however, a student and I reached an impasse. Tom felt that he deserved an A in science and I didn't agree. He failed to turn in a major project that was an important assignment for the quarter. He argued that he did all the work leading up to it, that he learned a great deal, and that the learning counted for something. I talked and he talked, but we couldn't agree. As a last resort, I suggested an arbitrator. I explained the role of an arbitrator and then suggested he choose someone from the class for that position. He chose his best friend, Earl. My heart sank. I felt that Earl would definitely side with Tom. Earl came out into the hall with us. We explained our problem; Tom told his position and I told mine. Earl thought a moment and then said, "Tom, if you feel deeply in your heart that you learned so much this quarter, that you worked so hard, and that you did the work, then give yourself an A. But if there is one doubt, then don't because you will have to live with yourself." I didn't know what to say. Earl left, and Tom and I agreed to meet the following morning. The next day, Tom said he felt he should get a B- because he didn't work as hard as he could have that quarter.

I was amazed at the wisdom of Earl. He asked Tom to examine his own thinking carefully, and I believe that having a peer respond in the role of arbitrator helped Tom clarify his thinking. This was the only time I've needed to have arbitration, and in this situation it worked well. It's something that I keep in the back of my mind for similar situations.

The first student-teacher conference can be a tense situation for some students; it is an unusual occurrence for most students. Usually the self-assured students will sign up first, becoming models for the rest of the class. I listen carefully, ask gentle questions, and offer encouragement. Then when the others see what the conference really is like, they feel more at ease. When all the student-teacher conferences are completed, the students are ready for the practice conference.

Practice Parental Conferences

With all the portfolios complete and report cards filled out, the students are ready for a practice parental conference. They've had an initial conference with me reviewing all the contents of the portfolio, and they have a basic idea of what they want to say to their parents. We take a few minutes and talk about organization. As a group we discuss what should come first and ways to efficiently organize all the information in the portfolio. The only request I have is that the report card be the last piece of information presented to parents since everything else in the portfolio supports the report card. After the first quarter, the students organize the portfolio contents on their own.

I want them to sail through the actual parent conference with ease and confidence. To help them do this, I arrange two important events: modeling a student-parent conference and scheduling a time for students to practice with other adults.

I've learned that students need to see a picture of what is expected of them during a conference. I pull in two other adults from the building to act as my parents for the modeling. The principal, secretary, librarian, and resource teacher have all been involved at one time or another. I grab anyone who happens by. I play the role of the student. My small acting group models two conferences with the first being a poor conference.

> ACT I: I enter the classroom leaving my "parents" behind. I don't even look at them or show them where to sit. I find my portfolio, toss it on the table, and slouch in a chair. My parents catch up to me and tentatively sit down. They are unsure of what to do. I finally push my portfolio toward them and tell them to look at it. The parents open the portfolio and attempt to make sense of all the paperwork. When they ask questions I answer with one-word answers. I never look at my parents, I comb my hair, and I play with my jacket zipper. I never touch my portfolio at all. When my parents are finished, I get up and leave the room while my parents are still sitting there. The students find this very funny and giggle all the way through the first act.

ACT II: I enter the room with my parents. I show them the picture bulletin board as we enter. I ask them where they would like to sit, and once they are seated I find my portfolio and return. I ask them if they would like some refreshments now or after the conference. Next I open my portfolio and begin sharing each page with them. I tilt the pages so that they can see the work and what I've written. I do the talking, answering questions and handling the papers. I use eye-to-eye contact and pay attention to the task. When I've finished I ask if there are any more questions. If not, I give a brief tour of the room, showing the work on the bulletin boards, the latest books on the shelf, and so on. Together, we leave the room.

After the miniplays are completed, we discuss their differences. I want them to realize that they are in charge of initiating the talk and that they control the portfolio contents. They are not passive participants but are the leaders. With the plays and discussion fresh in everyone's mind, they are ready for a practice conference.

The practice conference gives students the opportunity to explain everything to an adult (other than me) who is not a parent. I ask the adults I find to play the role of parents and to ask all the typical parent questions. During the practice conference, students practice their leading as they review their entire portfolio. Every time the students present what they know about themselves, the students are taking ownership of their learning (Weaver 1988). The practice conference builds confidence and the ability to discuss personal learning. After the practice conferences, students write about what went well and what they need to change for the student-parent conference. This is a final reflection and a time to consider the role of conference leader.

Last year, I invited university students to play the role of parents. When everyone was finished, I asked my sixth graders and the college students to write about the experience. Rick (a sixth grader) wrote,

> I felt nervous at first. As we went on I got better. I think I did a good job. I like the way I did it. I don't think I need to change anything. This was a good experience. Now I know how to do this.

After a conference with Jan (a sixth grader), a university student wrote,

> Jan is an extremely bright and talented individual. I'm impressed with her ways of thinking, and sophisticated behav-

ior. She is a very dedicated student who takes responsibility for herself and her grades. I was very impressed with how she claimed ownership of her own work, the good and the not-as-good. Not once did she try to "pass the buck" on to her teacher. She was very self-confident and really seemed to know what she wanted out of life. I was pleased with this interview and how this classroom worked.

Melissa (a sixth grader) wrote,

> I liked how the conference went. I didn't know the person I did it with, but she was very nice. I thought it was weird being in charge of the conference. I like being in control. If I did it again I would be more descriptive about my work and what I learned from it.

Her university listener wrote,

> One comment that will stay with me is this student's apparently proud explanation for the good grade she received in her hardest subject. She really felt she deserved it. Wonderful confidence.

Rose (a sixth grader) wrote,

> I thought it was fun. My "Mom" understood everything. I hope it goes that well with my real mom and dad. If I could change anything, I would make my Effort and Responsibility fast write more precise.

Another college student wrote,

> Jason walked me through his portfolio of work for the past quarter. He seems very confident about his work, and quite proud of the improvement he has made. As well he should be! I am very impressed with his ownership and pride in his work. Effort and responsibility were two words that rolled off his tongue so naturally. He really believes that what he is doing is important.

The students leave the practice conferences smiling and excited. They've accomplished a difficult task and are ready for anything. We hold one last class meeting to share successes and any concerns. Students often share the positive comments from their adult partners. Each time we reach this point, there is a strong feeling of accomplishment felt by all the students. Since we've done so much already, the rest will be easy. With this feeling of exuberance, we are ready for the parent conferences the next day. While leaving the class meeting, Anthony said, "Well, I was nervous, but I had everything I needed and I think I did good. Wish me good luck for tomorrow." We all did.

The Main Event: The Student-Parent Conference

In 1988, I climbed the Chilkoot Pass. Ulf, my German foreign exchange "son," climbed with me. I'm not an outdoors type of person, but I had wanted to climb the pass ever since I moved to Alaska. The Chilkoot Pass is the historic path the Klondike gold seekers used to reach the northern gold fields, and I guess I wanted to see if I was as rugged as they were. The climb, for me, signified being a "true" Alaskan. Ulf and I reached the bottom of the summit after the first day. As we pitched camp, I kept stealing glances at the cloud-covered pass. I kept wondering if I could reach the summit. That thought was still in my mind when we broke camp the next morning and headed upward. It was tough going. I crawled on my hands and knees over huge boulders. It was difficult and dangerous to stand upright because of the strong wind. The fog and mist hid the trail markers. I remember reaching a small plateau and finding a park ranger checking the climbers through. Ten minutes later, Ulf and I struggled over the top and headed downward. I'll never forget the feeling of accomplishment I had as I slid down the snowy slope. I remember thinking that I had really climbed the pass—and now I could do anything! I hummed and smiled to myself through the fog, wind, and blowing snow. My soaked boots didn't even bother me. The important thing was that I had done it. I did it!

I've seen students leave the evening of conferences with the same smile, the same humming, and the same feeling of accomplishment. All the preparation was the equivalent of my upward climb; the conference was like crossing the pass. They leave thinking "I did it." Self-esteem is almost always at a very high level that evening.

It's difficult to accurately describe everything that happens during the conference evening. The following is an excerpt from my journal as I recorded my observations during a second-quarter conference:

> The tablecloths are out, cookies arranged, lemonade cooling, and I'm eating supper—frozen yogurt. It's 5:45. Will they come? No matter how many times I do this, I always wonder if families will show up.
>
> At 5:50, Frank and his mom arrive early. He's all polished, clean shirt and hair combed. As she sits at a table by the window, he quickly finds his portfolio, joins her, and begins.
>
> At 6:00, the room fills quickly. Ruth and her mother drink lemonade while looking at the class photographs on the bulletin board.
>
> Chuck says, "Pick a table, mom." She picks one with a purple tablecloth. Chuck smiles and says, "Oh yeah, you like purple. Would you like some refreshments?" After his mother and brother are seated, Chuck goes to pick up cookies and drinks.
>
> Dennis and his father come in. Dennis's father is still in his military uniform. They find a table by the window. As Dennis shares his work, his father smiles. The father leans closer to Dennis, so they see the paper at the same time.
>
> Ruth and her mom laugh and giggle together as they read Ruth's reading log.
>
> With his mother sitting across from him, Chuck goes over each paper very carefully. Occasionally, she looks over Chuck's head and smiles at me.
>
> Greg and his mom speak Spanish as they look at the papers together.
>
> Ruth ends up in a fit of giggles. Everyone in the room turns to look and all smile at her laughter. Conversations then continue.
>
> Darrin's father rushed in with his family trailing behind. His father asks, "Mrs. Austin, what time are we?" "I scheduled the time wrong," Darrin apologizes. I say, "It's OK. There are no set times. Just find a table and begin." They stop at the refreshment table as Darrin finds his portfolio.
>
> When Johanna completes her conference, she takes her parents on a tour of the room. They look at the wire sculp-

ture on the bulletin board and the bug books on the shelf. The parents take time to glance through several.

I hear Greg explaining his summary sheet in Spanish.

Steve, his mom, and an unknown lady and child arrive. At the end of the conference I find out the woman is a neighbor who heard about "Steve's portfolio" and wanted to see it. So Steve invited her to his conference.

Darrin's mother catches my eye and smiles. She listens to Darrin read his fast-writes.

Hope takes her family on a room tour. They stop at the wire sculpture display and the reading chart. Hope explains that Ruth and Liz made a pop-up book as she shows her parents the published books. After reading several, the parents pull down the world map and check out the Middle East. On their way out the door, I talk with the family. They are very pleased with Hope's work. Her mom has tears in her eyes as she told me how proud she is of Hope.

Gradually the room empties and the sound of conversations softens. By 8:10 all the families are gone. Dave's family offers to stay and help clean up the room. We fold tablecloths, push desks back in place, and nibble leftover cookies. By 8:30 we are done, I turn off the lights, lock the door, and head home.

There are a great many activities happening at once during the conference evening, with families coming and going at different times. But the actual student-parent conferences include three critical participants. The first is the student who will lead the conference. The second is the parent who will be the primary audience for the child. And the third is the classroom teacher—me—who will be present but not actively participate in the conference. All three have very specific roles during the evening.

The Student's Role

This is the time the students have prepared for—their crossing of the pass. The student's role during the conference is to initiate, lead, and explain. At the first-quarter conference, many students begin by giving parents a tour of the room. That seems to be an easy way for students to enter the role of expert. Sharing the portfolio, then, is the logical next step. Later in the year, students vary this procedure by starting with the portfolio and then touring the room or offering refreshments.

Whichever way a student chooses, each one plans a definite way to begin their conference. They have their papers in order and know what they will say. From practice, the students know they lead the discussion about the contents of the portfolio, and they also know they will need to answer all the questions that arise.

Some students choose to sit between parents, while others sit facing them across the desk. In any position, however, the student is the one who handles the portfolio and its contents. The students keep the portfolio in front of them and share each piece of data individually. At her first conference, Jan knew exactly how she wanted to begin.

JAN: OK, first we begin with writing cause this is my best subject, reading and writing. We put both of them together, reading and writing. We had to xerox off some sheets—the first piece of writing we did and what we consider our best writing. And this I consider my best writing.

MOTHER: OK, read it.

JAN: OK. [*reading*] I am 35 years old, I live in the Virgin Islands and I have a husband and 2 children, a boy and a girl. I would be a medical doctor. I will start my day by being at work at 9:00 A.M. and work all day until 5:00 P.M. When I get home from work I'll cook for my family, do chores. Some days I may go shopping. When I get home, get ready for bed and get ready for work the next day.

FATHER: That's nice. Only thing is, doctor's hours are not that fast. Those are banker's hours, honey.

JAN: [*Jan giggles*] This is the first piece of writing that I ever did. We had to say something that touched our hearts. And this is a journal page.

Jan had an agenda in mind. She knew where she wanted to begin and how she planned to proceed through her portfolio. Charissa also plans her presentation as she determines the speed at which she shares her papers. She is the one who decides to wait for her father to finish reading one of her longer stories.

CHARISSA: Right here is my story. This is all my revision and stuff.

MOM: What is revision?

[*Charissa's father picks up the story and begins reading.*]

CHARISSA: You know when you revise and stuff, you have to scratch out things. Things that you misspelled and stuff. OK, I'll wait till

Dad's done. [*Charissa waits until he's finished.*] This took a lot of time. Every day we work, work, work.

Students also determine whether to orally discuss their work or read their fast-writes. Most do a combination of both, while a few (at least at the first conference) will primarily read.

Often during the course of discussion, the student identifies problems and gives possible solutions. During Jan's first-quarter conference, after sharing a science paper with her aunt and uncle, she stated, "If I would have double-checked my work, I wouldn't have gotten so many wrong. Since then, I have started to double-check my work." Anne also realizes what she needs to be aware of. Anne points out to her mother that "I have problems in making decimals line up and sometimes I add wrong, but in this case I got it right." Charissa already knows what she needs to do as she and her mother explore the reasons for a low grade in science.

MOM: Why do you have a D+ in science?
CHARISSA: Because I don't turn in all of my assignments.
MOM: Why don't you turn in all of your assignments?
CHARISSA: Probably because I don't do it or I don't write it in my assignment book.
MOM: So what are you going to do?
CHARISSA: I'm going to start turning in all my assignments and put my assignments in my assignment folder.

The student also decides when the conference is completed. The student concludes the conference by showing parents where to sign the report card. Pointing to the space on the report card, Charissa says, "You can sign anywhere right there. I have to keep part of this." She tears off the top copy. "Here you go. OK, this goes to you." She gives the top sheets to her parents. "And this is mine." She then takes bottom copy for her portfolio.

The Parental Role

The most vital task for parents is of course to attend the conference. At the conference, they need to listen carefully to what their child is saying, ask questions to clarify, collaborate on goals for the next quarter, and praise achievement. This all happens naturally within the sharing of the portfolio. At the first conference, the parents are a bit unsure of what is expected of them. But after the conferences begin, the parents relax and begin asking questions about papers, classroom procedures, or specific classroom vocabulary. The questions give the child an opportunity to venture off the practiced talk and respond in a natural way, as Anne does when she shares her insights about her reading book.

ANNE: OK. We had to choose some books and put a, do a fast-write with it. I chose *Bridge to Terabithia* as one of my books.

MOTHER: Chose what?

ANNE: *Bridge to Terabithia*. It's a really good book. Have you read it?

MOTHER: No, I don't think so. *Bridge to . . . ?*

ANNE: Terabithia. It's about this girl named Leslie and she had a best friend named, um, I forgot. Jess and, um, they were really good friends and Les was a girl and Jess was a boy. And she died, and um, she had this storm. There was this storm and they had to get to their fort on the other side of this creek or river. They had a rope attached to it and they were supposed to swing across and the rope broke and she fell in the river and cracked her head . . .

MOTHER: That's sad.

ANNE: During the storm. And I chose this book because it showed that friends, there are friends in the world and when one dies they are not really gone, they are in your heart and you also have your memories.

This is a natural conversation between parent and child about a book. While explaining the contents of the portfolio, other questions arise. Parents often ask questions about school procedures. Lon's mom wondered about book selection.

MOTHER: And how do you decide which book to read? Do you get to pick your own?

LON: Yeah, we just go over there to that shelf and see what looks good.

MOTHER: That's neat. Do you read every day? Does she give you a chance to read every day?

LON: Yeah, we read all the time.

MOTHER: Oh, that's neat.

In response to her father's questioning look, Charissa took time to explain the editing procedure.

Right here, see this is my piece. You always have to have an edit checklist. I'm an editor. There is an editor's box. You have a hat that says "editor" on it and no one can mess with you at that time. And you have sticky tabs. This is my first, second, and third [draft], because I haven't gotten to a final copy yet. And when you do that, right here is an editing checklist. "Author: Charissa Lowell. Title of Piece: Sleep Over Nightmare. Date: Jan 24, 1991. Written in pencil." You have to make sure all of this right, or if you don't the editing group cannot edit it. They cannot look through it and you have to take it back to them.

It's also not unusual for questions to arise about portfolio procedures as well. Parents are curious about how the child assembled the contents of the portfolio.

MOTHER: What is this?
ANNE: My summary sheet.
MOTHER: Oh.
ANNE: This is what Mrs. A though of me. [*Anne points to the teacher column on the summary sheet.*] And this is what Mr. Cook thought of me. [*Anne points to the next column.*] And this is what I thought. [*Anne points to the first column.*]

During Jan's conference, she explains the reason for the photocopied pages of reading books. "Right here, I had to choose two books that I learned from. From this one I learned that I liked poems and from this one I learned that you shouldn't cheat."

During the conference conversation, parents and child often find points of commonality. Anne was pleased that her mother had also read *Black Beauty* and knew Anne's favorite part in the book.

ANNE: The next book that I chose was *Black Beauty*.
MOTHER: And you have that book.
ANNE: Yeah.
MOTHER: Read it a million times.
ANNE: Yeah, I said I chose this particular book, *Black Beauty,* because it is interesting. I love horses and it shows you how to care for one, and it tells you how some people train horses. Here . . . like Black Beauty got really ill. You've read the book before, haven't you?
MOTHER: Yes.
ANNE: When he got ill?
MOTHER: I've read it several times, too.
ANNE: OK!

At the end of the conference as the child shares her report card, the parent and child have an opportunity to review the goals set for the next quarter. Parents seem to especially value this part of the conference. Often the child and parents clarify and extend the goal by discussing how to work on the goal at home and specific ways to reach the goal, which generally involves both the child and the parent. Jan and her aunt decide that "they both need to work on math." Jan will work at a more thoughtful speed and her aunt will spend time looking over the homework with Jan.

Before the conference officially ends, the student asks the parents to complete a parent reflection form. It's a blank sheet of paper with a place for the parent's name at the top with the words "My thoughts:" as a writing prompt. The purpose of the form is to provide a way for parents to offer their comments about the conference. I find that generally only one parent will write while the other suggests ideas. Comments often include a reflection on the entire conference and praise for their child.

The role of praise for the parents seems to follow naturally after the conference. The parents seem excited with their child's presentation and evidence of learning. After a conference evening, I noted in my journal that

> Soon there was only one family left. They continued to talk in low voices. With a smile, Steve closed his portfolio and returned it to the shelf. His father reached over and as he playfully messed Steve's hair he said, "I'm proud of you, son." Steve beamed and they walked out into the hallway together.

While Steve's father's reaction is fairly typical, once in awhile a parent doesn't fully believe all the information the student is sharing. The parent is interested in what the child has to say, but he feels the information is more accurate if heard from the teacher.

One year after the first-quarter's conference, Sandra's mother came over to me and asked me to come out in the hall and say something to her husband about Sandra. I followed the mother out of the room. Sandra's father asked, "How is she *really* doing?" I was totally surprised he would ask me that question as Sandra had just completed a very thorough forty-five minute conference. I realized that the father didn't yet accept Sandra in the role of an expert about her progress. I needed to find a way to answer this question without reducing Sandra's earned expert status and also model Sandra's new role to her father. The only thing I could think of doing was turning to Sandra and asking, "How do you think you are doing?" She replied that she thought she was doing just fine. "I agree with her," I said turning to her father. He was clearly confused. He wasn't quite ready to believe that his daughter could give an accurate picture of her own learning. He gave me a puzzled look and left. It wasn't until the third conference that he began showing trust in Sandra and her information. This is an extreme case, but it illustrates the fact that this is a new experience for parents. On the other hand, it's not a major problem for most. In fact, most parents are delighted with their child's ability to look at themselves as learners.

The Teacher's Role

I find my role during the conference to be very simple but very hard: Stay out of the conferences. I find a chair and sit. I refill the cookie tray or casually chat with parents as they leave. I talk with brothers and sisters of the students. But I do not wander or join students as they share their portfolios. Every time I come too close to an ongoing conference, the conference stops and looks to me as the ultimate one in charge. I don't want to do anything that undermines the credibility of the students as the experts on their own learning, so I stay out of the way. This is not to say that I can't join a conference if invited, but I'm very cautious when I am.

I've had parents and students invite me over to discuss an issue. Usually this happens when they discuss a goal for next quarter and parents want to know if it's realistic. During these times, I try to refer the question back to the student like I did with Sandra and her father, indirectly modeling for the parent to ask the child before asking me.

Another important job for me is encouraging the students. Throughout the evening, I continually support students quietly through smiles, eye contact, and nods of encouragement. Some students need this more than others. So as I'm trying to look busy but not intrusive, I keep an eye on the room and encourage when needed. I give lots of verbal praise and pats on the back when students finish. They've just crossed the pass. They've done it, and now they can do anything.

Continuing the Process, Taking the Next Step 4

❧The morning after the first conference, I am usually besieged with comments as the students burst through the classroom door. They all have a story to tell, and they all want me to listen. I've learned that it's important to take time to listen, so we settle as students share their conference experiences. While the students are remembering the night before, I'm already thinking about the next conference.

"Hiya, Mrs. A. Boy was I nervous at my conference last night, but after I started I was fine."

"Oh, Mrs. A, did you see my parents reading my story? They really liked it. My mom even laughed."

"Mrs. A, guess what? My parents and I went out for ice cream after the conference last night."

"Hey, did you see me last night? My conference lasted a long time. My parents kept asking questions. They didn't know what a fast-write was."

I want the students to carefully reflect on their actions during the conference with the purpose of identifying what went well for them and determining anything they need to change next time. I feel the need to capture their thoughts and impressions as soon as possible before the students lose them, so before we begin our daily routine, I ask the students to write.

I've structured this reflective writing several ways. I've asked students to write about what went well and what they would like to change. Other times, I've asked them to think about successes, about how the parent conference was different from the practice conference, or about what surprised them in the conference. I now have a more open format. I don't ask them to address specific ideas—I just ask them to write about the previous night. Whatever way I approach this, I find it important for the students to spend time thinking about the conference. It brings a formal closure to the process and provides a step toward the next conference.

Each student's writing is very different and mirrors their perception of their student-parent conference, but the writings seem to have three reoccurring elements. Students usually include a look at their feelings while leading the conference, elements of the conference they would like to change, and parent reactions during the conference.

Before her first conference, Allysa was nervous about the whole procedure. She was unsure if she could present her portfolio to her parents. The day after her first conference, she wrote,

> My conference last night went very well. We went through all of my work, and had a swell time. Except my little sister went to sleep at the table.
>
> The things that surprised me was that it wasn't as hard as I thought it was. When I had my conference with the practice, it was longer than with my parents.
>
> I feel very good cause I don't have to be nervous cause I've never done this before. After it was over I felt good cause I was scared at first. I wanted to get done as soon as possible. And that's how nervous I was. But next time it shouldn't be so hard.

Allysa is already thinking about her next conference experience. She sees that her next one will be easier since she's already completed one conference.

Aaron also wrote about being nervous during his first conference.

> It went fine. I was very nervous at first. Then I calmed down. It was pretty fun after that. What surprised me was my mom said she liked this kind of conference better. I feel great. I think this is the best kind of conference.

Even though Aaron was nervous, he finishes on a confident note. Like Allysa, he is ready to begin again.

A part of looking ahead to the next conference is for students to specifically reflect on the way they led the conference. Jan talks about her efforts to be in charge of the conference.

> Last night went very well for me. My aunt was very proud of my report card. I remembered that I had to present it

[the portfolio material] to her and I didn't just give it to her. We decided that we needed to work on math a little more. She was very impressed with my work.

Samantha looks at the same issue of leadership but in terms of organization.

Last night's reflection went great. My parents said that I did a great job on my report card and to keep it up. It went smoothly last night because I had no trouble on saying what I wanted to say. My portfolio was how I wanted to present it and I kept in order. I explained everything. At first I was shy and talked slowly and low.

Samantha's last sentence shows that she is aware of her speaking patterns. In a more direct way, Natalie reflects on her presentation delivery.

I think it went pretty well. The only thing that I have to work on is when I talk I always say um and I always stop and think what I'm going to say into the middle of my sentence. Other than that I think my conference was really done well.

The fast-writes often include comments about parents and their reactions during the conference. Students seem surprised both that parents are genuinely interested in hearing them talk about their learning and that parents aren't totally familiar with classroom terms and practices. After the third-quarter conference, Allysa wrote,

My conference went very good. He (my dad) asked a lot of questions, but I had all of the answers to them. We went through all of the papers and we discussed them for what problems I had. My parents think that it is a very good experience for us because it is teaching us how be very responsible students and it will help in the future.

Aaron also recorded his mom's reactions.

Well, my conference went well. My mom really enjoyed it. My mom liked to hear me talk and she loved my grades. She didn't really eat much. She loved my fast writes and the whole idea. I was really disappointed that my father could not make it.

Samantha was surprised with her father's reactions to the conference.

My conference went well. I knew what I was going to say. What surprised me was that how my dad reacted to my conference. He enjoyed it very much. The difference between practice conference and the real thing was that how more surprised my dad was and my dad let me do the talking and didn't ask many questions.

While Samantha's father didn't ask many questions, other students have seemed surprised that their parents do ask questions, that the students can be viewed as experts. Rose wrote,

The conference last night went great. My parents loved them. They said they were proud of me. When my mom asked what a fast write was I was surprised that she didn't know.

Melissa had the same reaction as Rose. In her writing, Melissa said,

It was very different than anything I've ever done before. It really surprised me that they (parents) had so many questions.

Another student wrote,

My parents read almost everything I had in front of them. They asked questions like "And what's that, what do you do with that, why, and what did you learn?"

Still another student wrote that

They were interested and they asked questions about my work. They listened and learned and watched.

The fast-writes help me gain a better understanding of how students perceive the actual conference. If there seems to be an overall problem or misperception, I can step in and help sort things out. While the students are busily writing, I am reading the parent reflection sheets. Their comments give me an overall view of the conferences from the parent community. Comments vary from blank pages to very short ("Very thorough, well prepared, and enjoyable—thank you!") to quite lengthy. One mother wrote,

I am impressed with this process in that it contributes greatly to Dennis's ownership of his own learning progress. That is significant, as academically, we know he's fine—but his maturity in the area of responsibility and care of his work reflect very adversely on his grades. Having him going through such an evaluation process has opened his eyes to the necessity of developing responsibility and best effort. As a result, he's evaluating his problem and developing solutions. That is wonderful!!

I read these comments carefully. I use them as a measure of how well the students are explaining their work and understand the whole conference process. If, for example, parents mention confusion about the effort and responsibility grade, I can make sure that we review that whole concept as a class and I can also address that topic in the weekly family letter. I also use this information to see where I need to increase personal contact with families. For the families that do not complete the reflection sheet, I ask their opinions about the conferences in the take-home journal. Some parents are more willing to respond in the take-home journals because it's a familiar arena. There are times, too, when parents have to leave for work and don't have time to write, or the parent reflection sheet somehow becomes overlooked. The take-home journal offers those parents another opportunity to respond to the conference evening. For the parents who don't respond, and there are usually only one or two in the classroom, I don't pursue the issue after the first contact. I do try to generally chat with them when they attend any school event, but never about conferences. I want the parents to feel comfortable participating in school events, so when they do come I don't want to challenge them. I believe that when they feel at ease, they will then be more willing to write their opinions.

Another source of information is my observational notes. When I first began student-parent conferences, I sat and took observational notes. I don't do that anymore since I found that it intimidated the students and the parents. Now I write my impressions after the families leave. I try and notice relationships between students and parents. I look at body language, voice tone, facial expressions, and so on. I record anything I feel is significant in planning for the next conference. After one conference I wrote,

> Dennis's father came. I never met his father before. Dennis showed his father his work and his father smiled as he read the paper. The more Dennis shares, the closer his father leans. The father asked many questions and Dennis seemed to be able to answer them.
>
> Greg and mom talked in Spanish. (I didn't expect that.)

Michelle's mom called me over to explain something I wrote in the narrative.

Layla arrived with mom. Mom didn't look happy. Layla took a deep breath as she began. Did just fine. Mom relaxed. Positive ending.

When I look at my notes, I might realize that I need to make very sure Michelle understands everything by setting up an extra practice time for her. Or perhaps it looks like Layla needs more confidence, and I need to talk more about this process in the take-home journal to her mother. I was also glad to hear Greg and his mom talking in Spanish. That tells me they are both comfortable in the room. I need to write to Dennis's father in the take-home journal. It's the first school event he has ever attended, and I'd like to encourage his participation.

As I continue to review the student writing, the parent comments, and my notes, I formulate a plan for next quarter. I am constantly thinking of ways to make the process clearer and easier for the parents and students. It is never the same from year to year. Each class is so different, and this process requires tailoring to fit each one.

An interesting phenomena that happens the day following the conferences is the change within the classroom, especially after the first one. It's difficult to describe, but there three distinct and different feelings on that day. The first is a strong feeling of camaraderie—like we climbed the mountain together and planted our flag. The second is celebration—we can all rejoice and enjoy last night's accomplishments. The third is relief. Preparing portfolios takes time and thinking, and the students are glad they completed the task.

The student's writing and actions reflect these three emotions, but I first notice the changes in the students' actions. There was a different feeling in the classroom after we do conferences for the first time. There is a closeness among the students that wasn't there before. They have shared a strong common experience that unified them. Johnson and Johnson (1984) point out that in an effective group, "cohesion needs to be high." The conference provides a cohesive experience that becomes a part of our class history—stories to be told and retold throughout the year. The camaraderie attitude was evident in the actions of the students. Each has a story to share and everyone listens carefully. Conferences also provide a leveling aspect. Everyone participates and so everyone has similar experiences. It's the we're-all-in-this-together attitude.

The attitude carries over into the feeling of celebration. The day after a conference has the satisfying feeling of something done well. This confidence is very strong. Rose wrote,

> Last night went well. My mom understood all of my work. My mom said she was very proud of me. These conferences are better than the ones last year because no matter what your grade they are proud of you.

So we relax and do celebrate. We talk, write, smile, and enjoy each other's company. We all feel tired, but it's a good kind of tired. We spend the day after conferences reflecting and preparing for the next quarter.

Students file the contents of their conference portfolio in a cabinet in the back of the room. We save these for the last quarter, where we examine our learning for the whole year. They store their empty conference portfolios in a box in the corner and begin a classroom portfolio for the next quarter. These will hold all the papers for the next nine weeks.

Each student has identified a personal goal for next quarter, either an academic or social goal. It should be the *one* thing they want to focus on in the next nine weeks. They then copy their goal onto a half sheet of construction paper and tape it to the inside of their desk. This allows them to see it every time they open their desk.

We follow this reflective process after every conference experience except for the last one. The last conference is different because it's a review of the learning for the entire year.

In preparation for the final student-parent conference, the students really prepare for two different aspects of the same meeting. They share with parents the learning that has taken place in the last quarter as well as review the whole year's growth and learning. Since the majority of the students are very familiar with the reflective process, I find that they have little difficulty in preparing both sections. The end-of-the-year review also brings closure to the entire year and helps students and parents see the changes that have taken place. I've structured this procedure in different ways over the years depending on the class and my thinking at the time. I always begin the same way, however, by having the students review the contents of all four of the conference portfolios.

After the students finish preparing the usual conference portfolio, we begin looking together at the entire year. We push the desks back and spread out. The students then take all four of the conference portfolios and carefully examine and compare the contents. They especially look at the large summary sheet from each quarter. Since it is a summary of four different views, it offers a very comprehensive review of the year. After spending considerable time looking at all the information, the students find a classmate to talk with about their observations. This talking is important to the process, allowing the students to put their thoughts into words. They often gain new ways of thinking about the information from their partner.

I first begin by asking students to do a year's summary fast-write on each subject by identifying the changes that have occurred over the year. I ask them to consider what they can now do that they couldn't when they first walked in this room. Gary pulled out all his information concerning math. He looked at the papers he included in the four portfolios: his writing about math, his effort and responsibility writing, his actual math papers, my comments, and his parents' perceptions of him as a math student. He then wrote the following:

> I have improved in math by learning how to divide fractions, multiply to the second power. I have learned so much it is hard to keep it all straight. I have really changed by the way I look at math. Last year Math was my worst subject. I hated math, but this year Math is my favorite subject. When I was in 5th grade multiplication was my enemy. This year it is my friend.

Another way I've asked students to reflect on the year is to concentrate only on the values we've identified as important, such as effort and responsibility. Again the students examine the entire contents of all of the conference portfolios but with an emphasis on how they've changed in effort and responsibility. In writing about effort, Rose said,

> I feel I have learned that I wasn't going to have someone to pick up after me bringing my homework to school for me or putting my name on my paper. I feel that I have never really thought about how much I have learned, if I stop to think I feel I have grown greatly as a learner, such as turning in my homework and listening to the speakers and showing interest in what they are saying, because if I were talking I would as you would wish they do to you.

Dennis combined effort and responsibility into one piece of writing and also looked toward the next school year.

> I learned no matter how hard you try you don't always win. I have been trying all year to grow in responsibility. I have

grown in responsibility and many other things. I feel it is
good that I've tried, but I wanted to reach a higher goal in
responsibility. I have learned to be successful by becoming
a person who puts all his effort into his goals. I think I
could try much more to reach goals. My most main goal is
to become responsible. I will try to continue my growth in
responsibility. I will not stop trying to reach my goals until
I have reached them, then I can set higher goals. I will start
off next year with a goal and reach it or keep trying to. I
am not going to sit around and hope for the best.

The other way I've structured the year's review is for the students
to chose the most significant learning event of the year for them in each
subject. To do this, they critically review everything we've discussed
during the year in each subject and their work that they chose in their
conference portfolios to represent them as learners. Melissa chose the
simulated oil spill activity for science.

In science, I think the most important "hands on" science
thing we did was the oil spill. On the "beach" that our group
made was a couple of shells, chips of wood, and feathers.
Half of the tray was water. On the water we put a boat we
made, punched holes in it and poured oil in it. The oil
spilled out of the boat. It got into the water and all over
the beach. We had to clean up the oil spill. We learned how
the workers felt when they helped clean-up oil. It made us
realize something that we didn't really understand.

Last year, I felt strongly that the students should help decide how
to do go about structuring the year's review, so we held a class meeting.
The class decided to divide into groups of four, come up with sugges-
tions, and then report back to the whole group. After much vigorous
talk, one group suggested that we fast-write on important things learned
during the year. Another group felt we should examine how we've
grown as learners in each subject. A third group decided that a long
written paper on what we've learned would cover it all. The last group
suggested we write down all the things covered and then students could
write about one that they learned the most from. After much discussion
the class finally decided.

AUDREY: I think we should do a fast-write on what was the most
important thing learned in that subject all year.
ROSE: But there were lots of important things, not just one thing.

MRS. A: What would you suggest?

ROSE: I don't know.

HUGH: Include all other portfolio papers. Pick the one that you learned the most from and then do a fast-write on that.

AARON: I agree with Rose, there are lots of important things, but we can't write on them all. Let's chose the one that we learned the most from.

So we did. As always, when the students help make the decisions and plans they are much more involved. Since this is work in addition to the preparation for the conference portfolio, I've found that the students need to be involved in ways that complete the process. Out of all the ways I've tried to work the end-of-the-year review, I prefer this one and will continue having students decide the way they want to review the year.

On the night of the final student-parent conference, the students first share their portfolios for the last quarter and then they share their review of the year. They are done; they have completed a whole year involved in examining themselves as learners. In *Seeking Diversity*, Linda Rief (1991) writes, "The act of putting together a portfolio is a reflective act in itself, as students choose what to put in there and why. That reflection on where they've been, where they are now, and how they got there is what real learning is all about" (45). I want my students to have such "real learning."

Reflections 5

For me, the last day of school is like New Year's Eve. It's a time to sadly say good-bye to my students who have become copartners in learning, to pack the classroom contents in brown boxes, to pull the shades and lock the door. It's also the time I carefully reflect on the past school year. I go home and sit out on my back porch with a bowl of cherries, my feet propped up, and watch the squirrels tease my two dogs. I think about the year. What went well? What do I need to change? How can I make it easier? While these are questions that I continually ask myself throughout the year, summer break provides the time to reflect, read, and play with possibilities. So, with propped-up feet and a bowl of glistening cherries in my lap, here are the ideas that I'm currently pondering.

Subject Integration

A situation arose this year that forced me to think about the consequences of the integration of subject areas. As the classroom became more and more subject integrated and unit themes took hold, the students and I found that often one project encompassed many subject areas. Since the report card is broken down into subject areas, specific grades *must* be given in each of those areas. Sam really brought this to my attention when he asked if he could use a Greek column drawing done in art for math in his portfolio since it was the first time he measured accurately on the initial try. I realized that I could not dictate the specific learning experiences for individual students as students learn different things in the same activity. I still haven't resolved this problem. The students and I could decide as a class under which subject to classify each project or paper and majority rules, or we could consider a project part of every subject in which it applies. For instance, the column art project would be counted in art, math, social studies, and reading. I have no final solution as yet. This may be an issue the students and I work out together next year.

Time

Time is another issue that I always think about. How can I streamline the process to make it easier and more efficient? Someone suggested that I give students examples of reflective fast-writes so that the preparation for the first-quarter conferences doesn't take so long. I've considered that option, but I know that if I did that many students would copy the language of the models and not think for themselves.

Another time issue concerns my teacher narratives. They take a lot of effort and time and, aside from using the address labels for notes, I'm always looking for a faster and more efficient way to write them. I've eliminated the idea of a computer program that allows me to insert the name and then select phrases that fit a form letter since the letters are meant to be personal and that wouldn't really be personalized. Terry Johnson told me about teachers in British Columbia who write specific types of narratives, such as a narrative focused on one subject or one criteria such as social behavior or a vignette of a classroom happening and the significance of the child's role. I'm not sure how this would fit into the idea of the summary sheet. Would writing shortened or more-focused narratives be meaningful to the student? Maybe this is one area where efficiency is not the most important aspect to be considered. Instead of writing the narrative, I think I might experiment with taped conferences with individual students. I'd like to know if talking directly to each student would be more helpful than the written letter. I would still use all my notes and records, but it might take less time. I would have to think carefully about the management of these taped conversations.

Storage and Filing

Paper management continues to be a concern, too. While everything is held in a filing cabinet or in boxes, I would like to figure out a way to make the process a bit more orderly and streamlined. The large pictures often get bent in storage. As I gain more technical equipment, like a computer, TV, VCR, and overhead projector, the room to store everything decreases. Currently I don't have solution, but I will continue thinking.

This leads to another thought—I have come to suspect I have too much of an emphasis on paper-and-pencil activities as the substance of the portfolio. At the end of the first quarter last year, Cecilia asked if she could use a partner activity instead of choosing a specific math paper. She said that she learned how to use a math reference book from her partner. So I'm thinking that next year, students will have the choice to include paper-and-pencil work along with other activities that don't have specific written results.

One thing I do know that I want to do is to prepare a professional portfolio. I did this on a limited basis this year, but I would like to be more consistent and have one for each quarter. I learned that choosing items that reflect me as a learner and a professional was difficult. I now better understand the dilemma some students have in choosing items to include. Also, I found that my professional life and home life were often intertwined and I would like to strengthen this awareness in the minds of the students. The values that we identify for the classroom—effort and responsibility—could be reflected upon within the home context as well. After my portfolio preparation I better understand the need to share the contents. My husband was out of town during our conferences and I desperately wanted to share with someone, so I spread my portfolio out on a table in the hallway during the conference evening for parents and students to examine. I felt so excited when a family paused at the table. Sharing my learning allowed me to be an active participant in the evening. This idea might be expanded to include parents as well. In the invitation to the conference, students could ask their parents to be prepared to share something they've learned recently. This could be strong modeling for the child if parents cooperated. It would make the evening a celebration of everyone's learning, not just the learners in the classroom.

I've also been thinking about technology such as computers and videos. Maybe this problem will take care of itself as technology naturally falls into projects. Cameras of all types are natural vehicles to record those non-paper-and-pencil projects and results as they have the potential of providing a vivid picture of the student. I just don't know how to manage all the details yet.

The dogs have given up on the squirrels and are now sleeping in the shade. Finishing up the cherries, I think about the journey my students and I have taken in the last six years. I had set out to find a way to make assessment more meaningful to students. I wanted them to assume more responsibility, to see connections between effort and learning, and to become actively involved in their own learning. After carefully examining numerous audio- and videotapes of conferences, surveys of students and parents, interviews, class discussions, my observational notes, other teacher's experiences and comments, and student writings, I know that student-parent conferences meet my expectations.

I think of Rose, Allysa, Phillip, Charissa, Ruth, and the rest who grew to realize the importance of work in relation to personal success. Of Jake and Cecilia, whose successes—no matter the size—were applauded by the entire class community. Of Ron, who grew to value himself. Of Ann, Melissa, Johanna, Miles, John, and others who struggled to view themselves with an honest eye and left sixth grade with a balanced and positive picture of their abilities. Of Aaron and Jerry and Sandra, who gained additional parental respect. And of all the others who learned the value of personal responsibility, trust, and community support. After six years of student-parent conferences, I can see that the important implications of my research results aren't in the sweeping generalizations but in the individual students. The student-parent conferences make a difference to them depending upon their own needs.

As I eat my last cherry, I look forward to beginning again in the fall, to trying out new ideas and seeing where they lead, to watching how students adapt the idea of conferences to fit their personalities and perspectives, and to observing the students become independent, active, and assertive learners. I can't wait.

Final Notes on Management: Fitting the Pieces Together

6

When I share student parent conferences with other teachers and after they've seen and heard examples, the same question is always asked. How does everything fit together? This chapter addresses that concern. I talk about where I begin and what I do next, how to keep the class together and yet finish on time. These issues are separated from the rest of the text for easy reference so that as you are in the middle of conference preparation, you will be able to return to the mechanics of the process easily and quickly.

Every summer about a month before school starts I begin to dream about school. It's always a similar dream: I dream of being in front of a class and not remembering why I am there. The children are out of control, the intercom calls me to the office, a parent wants to see me in the hall, the lunch count is due, and a new student has just arrived. I stand there not knowing what to do first. I always wake up before I solve this dilemma. The management of student-parent conferences can seem like this dream. Portfolios need to be constructed, parent forms created, grades given to students, practice sessions scheduled, personal narratives written. What do I do first? How do I keep all the students together so that we all finish by the conference date?

I've worked out a system over the years but, like everything else, it's constantly changing and evolving. I do know that if I'm going to guide the students through a year successfully, I need to have a very clear map of where we are going. Each fall, I sit down and think about the successes of last year, the changes that need to be made, and the new ideas yet to be tried. I consider what the best ways to allow students to reflect on their own learning are. What is needed in the portfolio to show reflection? What is the simplest and most effective way for students to obtain information about their learning? What kind of organizational techniques would help in the student's presentation? The management plan that I've developed includes three stages: weekly groundwork, conference preparation, and conference night.

Weekly Groundwork

My primary role in laying the groundwork of student-parent conferences involves communication to both the students and the parents. The students' role is to begin to see themselves as capable of participating in the assessment process as reflective learners.

Classroom Portfolios

If students are to adequately reflect on themselves as learners, they need the proper data. One way for them to reflect is to collect all their work in a classroom portfolio. Each student has a legal-sized manila folder that is kept in a filing cabinet in the back of the room. Other teachers use milk crates, boxes, or trays. The students keep all of their work in the folders and none of it goes home unless requested by the parents. If parents wish to see the student's work, the papers are sent home on Friday and returned on Monday. The purpose of these rules is to have data for the students to reflect on their learning, and the students aren't aware of which papers are important until they begin to prepare for a conference.

Paper Management. Management of these papers can be chaotic. My goal is to have all the student papers filed in their classroom portfolios in an efficient manner. I've tried several different ways to accomplish this. I first tried passing back papers on a daily basis and having each student file their own, but this took too much classroom time. Then I tried having a filing committee. Their job at recess was to file all the papers in each folder. This eliminated the use of class time, but too many papers were misfiled and the students didn't have the opportunity to see the papers again (they've already graded the papers themselves). Currently I'm using a "bin" system. After the students grade their papers, I record the grades and then I put them in a yellow bin. On Friday, two students pass out the classroom portfolios, then five students take about fifteen minutes to pass back all the papers from the yellow bin. As the students receive a paper, they classify it and clip it to a labeled sheet of paper according to its specific subject area: language arts, math, science, social studies, art, or computers. When it's time to begin to prepare for student-parent conferences, the classroom portfolio is quite full and the students have many papers to chose from.

There are some items or events that don't fit the file folders, like pieces of art or major projects. The larger papers are kept in a cardboard box tucked away in the coat closet. Other teachers tape pieces of posterboard together to create a larger type of file. For projects, performances, athletic events, student council speeches, and so on, a Polaroid camera provides a visual record.

Lists of Concepts Learned

As the students are passing out portfolios and papers, others are creating lists of concepts learned during the week on the chalkboard. I list the subject areas across the top of the board and students brainstorm all the activities, topics, or ideas discussed under the appropriate subject. As the students organize their papers, I type the lists on the computer. By the end of the quarter, we have a very extensive overview of our learning that students can use when preparing their portfolios.

Communication with Parents

Weekly Letters and Take-home Journals. While the students are organizing their data, I am in constant communication with the parents. In chapter 2, I shared the idea of weekly letters, take-home journals and back-to-school night. For student-parent conferences to be totally successful, I have to be in consistent contact with parents. This takes time, but I feel the rewards are well worth it. The weekly letters are sent home every Friday and I usually write and photocopy them before school on Friday morning. The take-home journals take longer to do since I usually have twenty-eight to answer. The journals go home with me on Thursday night, and it takes about an hour and a half to write in all of them. The amount of writing varies depending on the week, the student's activities, parent responses, and my energy level. I try to balance these out by not having anything else to work on that evening. I plan work on Thursday that doesn't need my immediate attention and activities on Friday that don't require heavy preparation. It doesn't always work out this way, but I try to use these guidelines.

The Student Performance. The next step in parent communication is inviting the parents into the school for some type of student performance and using that opportunity to explain student-parent conferences. But before I explain everything to the parents, I first introduce the idea more fully to the students. I do this through a class meeting.

My talk usually begins by me saying something like "We're kind of a different class, aren't we? Let's think of all the special things we do together." The students usually mention singing in the morning, overnight camping trips, cooking, walking to the library, working in groups, performances, and so on. "We do a lot of different things," I say. "Why do you think we do them?" They often note that we're special or lucky or hard workers or that we're responsible. I say,

> We are all those things, but most of all, all of you are responsible students. You are bright and hard working and I like to learn new things with you. Today, we will begin thinking about another new project—student-parent conferences. Our conferences will be different, because in these conferences you will be talking with your parents. I won't be involved.

At this point, the students gasp a bit and I spot panic in their eyes. I look at them and ask, "Wait a minute: Have I ever asked you to do something that you couldn't do?" They shake their heads.

> Then hang in there. Wait till you hear about this before you make up your mind. First, I wouldn't just tell you to do this and leave you. We'll work on this together like we do everything else. We'll help each other and we'll practice so much that by the time conferences arrive you'll be very confident. Besides, you are the best qualified people to share what you've learned. You're the experts. You'll be great, just wait and see. Your parents will be amazed with what you can do.

The meeting ends with lots of questions about what all this entails. Now that the students have a idea of what is expected, I share the same details with the parents after the student performance.

I plan the student performance evening around the end of October—before the holiday rush begins and when parents don't feel so frazzled. The kind of performance varies each year. It's been as elaborate as a fully staged musical to as simple as a choral reading. It all depends on the time available and the strengths of the class. I purposely wait until October to introduce the idea for many reasons. First, the conference time is closer and so the reason to know is more important and not as easily forgotten. Second, the students and I have been together long enough for the students to know more about our classroom vocabulary and procedures—things like saving papers in portfolios and the terms *self-assessment* and *reflection*. The students are then able to answer some parent questions about assessment already. Third, the parents and I have had a chance to get to know one another, build a working relationship, and establish an element of trust. In my communications with parents to date I've continually reinforced the idea of personal student responsibility. And fourth, I can include the new students that have joined us since September.

After the performance, when the applause dies down and students are seated with their parents, I talk about student-parent conferences. During the question time, I encourage students to answer as many of the questions as they can. This again models to parents that their child can be seen as an expert in the assessment process. I am continually working to change parent perceptions so that they think of their child as capable of self-assessment. After this question-and-answer session, I have a better idea about which parents and/or students need more information about the process or need more support in accepting this type of conference.

Conference Preparation
Specific Contents of Conference Portfolios
About halfway through the first quarter, I begin to think seriously about the specific contents of the conference portfolio. This is an important part of my plan; I need to be very clear about my expectations. I've discovered that the clearer I am in my mind and the better picture I have, the easier it is for the class. I begin with three initial questions: What are the best ways to allow students to reflect on their own learning? What is needed in the portfolio to show reflection? What is the simplest and most effective way for students to obtain information about their learning? I make a list concerning the contents of the conference portfolio.

Purpose, Procedure, and Participant. For each item that will be included in the conference portfolio, I reflect on the purpose of the piece of data, the procedures for obtaining the information, and the role of the participant in using that data.

1. Purpose. Stating the purpose of each piece requires me to articulate the reason for including that particular piece in the conference portfolio. Everything must have a reason for being there.

2. Procedure. This is made up of notes to myself on how best to obtain that piece for the portfolio.
3. Participant. This is the students' role. I begin thinking about what the students will need to do. Where possible, I write a sample student response. While I don't show the sample to the students, the writing requires me to clarify my thinking.

My list last fall looked like this:

1. Self-selected papers
   Purpose:
   >   shows evidence of learning
   >   for self-examination and self-reflection
   Procedure:
   >   student chooses own papers
   >   select two papers from each subject area
   >   select one from art
   >   select one piece of writing
   >   select one reading log page
   >   select one daily journal page
   Participants:
   >   Think about "What represents me as a learner?" and
   >   "What did I learn from this paper?"
2. A fast-write about each chosen paper
   Purpose:
   >   focusing thoughts into a concrete written text
   >   constructing a precise vocabulary about learning
   Procedure:
   >   use one sheet of paper for each fast-write, which allows for easier organization of portfolio
   Participants:
   >   include reason for choosing paper
   >   be precise
   >   don't use global terms such as "good" or "I learned a lot"
   Example
   >   I chose this math paper, because at first I didn't know when to reduce fractions. I worked hard on it, but I couldn't figure it out. By the time I did the second math paper, I understood how to do it. I now know to look for even numbers, numbers ending in five or zero, or to count by multiples.

3. Student Observation Sheets
    Purpose:
        gives three perspectives of student as learner
        shows parent their input is valued
        allows me to voice my opinion
        additional teacher feels part of assessment process
        shows student that learning takes place everywhere
    Procedure:
        parent and other teacher complete forms
        I write narrative to student
    Participant:
        student asks for form to be completed
        student picks up completed form

4. Grade Graph
    Purpose:
        gives a visual picture of work for each subject
        student can compare self to average range
    Procedure:
        one graph for each subject
    Participants:
        record daily grades and tests in each subject
        construct bar graph
        average own grades three times

5. Summary Sheets
    Purpose:
        student awareness of others' view of them as learners
        internalize perceptions of others
    Procedure:
        summarize information from observation sheets
    Participants:
        complete summary sheets
        use own words to record information

6. Effort and Responsibility
    Purpose:
        reflect on effort and responsibility in each subject
    Procedure:
        write one reflection for each subject area
        use one sheet of paper for each (easier organization)
    Participants:
        be precise

give examples, back up what you say

can use concept circles on the wall

grade self

Example:

In social studies, I was not that responsibile this quarter. I did complete my ancient explorer project, but I didn't study for my map tests. I got five low grades. But I always turned in my homework. I did OK in effort. I practiced my report to the class, but again I didn't study. I feel I should get a 70 percent in effort and responsibility.

7. Grades

Purpose:

reach a conclusion by reflecting on data

Procedure:

examine contents of portfolio

Participants:

average grade graphs and effort and responsibility grades in each subject

Preparation Time

With my vision fairly clear, I'm ready to begin. If it's the first quarter, I allow about two weeks, spending most of the day preparing for the conferences. Since this is a totally new concept for the students, it's important for them to thoroughly understand each step. Understanding each step includes time for talking, rehearsing, and rewriting. Two full weeks are a considerable length of time to spend on assessment. In the beginning I worried about the time involved. However, after carefully examining all the actions of the students, I've decided there is no better way for them to practice skills such as summarizing, editing, reflecting, averaging, and critical thinking. Preparation time does diminish after the students are familiar with the process. The second time, it usually only takes a week. Three days is the average time spent preparing the portfolio for the third and fourth quarters. One primary teacher after the first quarter only uses the afternoons for portfolio preparation. After initially introducing the portfolio idea to the whole class during the first quarter, several primary teachers use centers as a way of compiling the portfolio. Each center focuses on one aspect of the portfolio. For example, a center would be set up for creating the grade graphs while another would have the math folders for students to choose their math papers. The first quarter does take the longest preparation time, but once the students are familiar with the process and purpose, they can prepare most of their portfolio on their own.

The Conference Portfolio. The first step toward preparing is for students to make a new portfolio—the conference portfolio. They decorate a legal-sized file folder. Not only does the decorating create ownership, but it is also easier to identify when they are spread out on the table on conference night. Using brightly colored paper, they also create separate subject divisions for their portfolios.

As they finish up the decorating, I list the first day's requirements on the board:

1. Choose *two* papers from each subject.
> Think about:
> How does this reflect me as a learner?
> What did I learn from this?
> Clip with subject heading paper.

2. Do a fast-write for each paper chosen.
> Address:
> Why did I choose this paper and how does this reflect on me as a learner?

3. Edit with a partner.
> Think about:
> Does this make sense?
> Is it precise?
> Watch out for spelling and punctuation.

4. Copy in ink *neatly.*

5. Clip each piece of writing behind its subject heading paper.

6. Make an invitation for your parents.
> Use color.
> Include all the information listed on the back board.
> Include RSVP.
> Edit with a partner.

7. Fast-write about effort and responsibility.
> Write one fast-write for each subject area.
> Be precise.
> Give examples.
> Use charts on the wall for vocabulary, if needed.
> Give grade in each subject.
> Edit with a partner (check #3).
> Copy in ink *neatly.*

We review these instructions together and then the students proceed at their own pace, helping each other when needed.

The next day, I again review the list on the board, erase the steps that *all* students have completed, and add:

8. Construction of grade graphs.

> Label graph for each subject.
> Create average area (70–79 range)
> Color light blue.
> Make bar graph.
> Color bars.

9. Photocopy these items, which should reflect you as a learner.

> Think about: How does this reflect me as a learner?
> One page from two different books you've read.
> One page from your reading log.
> One daily journal page.
> One piece of your writing.
> Sign up on the board when you have all of this ready.

10. Fast-write for each item in #9.

> Address: Why did I choose this paper and how does this reflect me as a learner?
> Edit with a partner.
> Copy in ink *neatly*.

As students work through the list and sign up on the board, they go by twos with *all* their selections to the work room. We don't have time for students to make additional trips to the copying machine, so they need to have all their selections ready before they go. A parent volunteer supervises the copying so the procedure can be done quickly and efficiently.

Grade and Portfolio Reviews. While this is happening, I begin sharing the grades recorded in the grade book. I ask that students have all the graphs prepared before I come to their desk, which means they need to have the subject title, the average range colored in, and numbers along the vertical axis. I go to each student and read off the recorded grades. As I read them aloud, the student writes them in ink along the horizontal axis. I ask them to use ink so there is no question of any changes. This sharing of grades gives the student and me an opportunity to talk. The student can ask questions about a specific grade or problem with the portfolio, and it gives me an opportunity to personally check with each one. I often point out something that a parent might ask about—"Your mom is probably going to ask you about this. What are you going to say?" I'm modeling for the student to look ahead and think about what parents might want to know. The sharing of grades, coupled with conversation, usually takes me about an hour or so for twenty-eight students.

Summary Sheets. The next couple of days are for everyone to catch up. Those students that are done help the others by editing, assisting with grade graphs, and organizing papers. When we are all caught up, we begin the summary sheets.

The summary sheets take the longest and are, I think, the hardest single written aspect for students to do. For this reason, we begin a new day with this task. On the board I write,

1. Summary sheets
> Please do in order:
> Fill in your reflections first.
> Fill in your parent's reflections.
> Fill in additional teacher's reflections.
> Fill in Mrs. A's reflections.
> Edit with a partner and correct.
> Think about: Does this make sense?

Together we practice doing this. I create an imaginary student and we look at all the information from parents, me, and the other teacher. On the overhead, we complete a summary sheet for that student. The modeling is a good review for some students and provides a way to begin for others. Some students spend a long time working with partners on this part of the portfolio.

Final Tasks. As they are working on the summary sheets, I write on the board the final tasks in preparing the portfolio.

2. Average Grade Graphs
> Use calculators.
> Average until you get the same answer three times.
> Have your partner do the same.
> Write the average on back of each grade graph.

3. Final Grade
> Use calculators.
> Average effort and responsibility grade with graph grade.

Do the same for each subject.

Have your partner do the same.

Put final grade in a circle on the bottom of the effort and responsibility fast-write.

4. Organize portfolio for conference with Mrs. A.

The students that complete their portfolios first move on to help others. My feeling is that none of us are done until all of us are done. Last year, Paul was having problems organizing all his papers. Kris, Stephanie, and Carrie sat down with him and helped him put his portfolio together. Chuck, a new student during the third quarter, was having difficulty keeping up with the class during preparation week. Carl and David "adopted" him and showed him the routine. Chuck, in turn, showed another new student, Sara, during the fourth quarter. Because the feeling of community has been an integral part of the classroom, helping each other is a normal expectation. With portfolios complete, individual conferences begin.

Individual Student Conferences

On the days of the individual conferences, I plan the class activities carefully. As I meet with a student in the back of the room, the others are completing portfolios or helping others to do so. If there is no one to help, then I list tasks on the board for students to complete. As in any normal classroom, there are always a few students that need more structure, so I plan for this ahead of time. It's important for students to realize that a student and I can't be interrupted during a conference. On average, it takes about two days to meet with twenty-eight students. If there were interruptions, we would never finish.

The students come back to me in the order they've signed up on the board. During the conference, we review their portfolio and, if it's incomplete in any way, I ask the student to return to their seat and make the necessary corrections. I look for precise language in the writing—not "I did good in math"—as well as for all of the components to be organized in a coherent manner and for evidence of editing. It's not unusual for some students to redo parts of their portfolio two or three times. Often I will refer them to another student for additional help and explanation.

Also during the conference with me, students complete their own report card. As we discuss each subject, they write the agreed-upon grade in the correct space and then complete the rest of the card. At the first conference, I explain what each section means and how to fill it in.

When we finish, students return to their seats and organize their portfolios one last time before the practice conference the following day.

The Practice Conference

I've tried a variety of approaches with this stage. I began by begging and cajoling my colleagues—the reading teacher, special education teachers, librarian, and so on—to listen to student conferences throughout the day as they have time. The advantage of this method is that the listeners are in the building and available. The disadvantage is that the teachers give up their already limited time to work with my students. Plus, it takes a long time to complete the practice conferences. One year, I invited personnel from the central administration to come and listen. The biggest advantage of that option is that they are totally new people for the student to talk with, but the disadvantage of using them is that because of their schedule, they can't come on a regular basis and their numbers are limited. Shirley Kaltenbach uses a few parent volunteers as listeners, while Karen Mitchell uses primary grade teachers to listen to conferences that are scheduled after school.

I now invite education students from the local college to act as parents, and I've found this to be the best approach for me so far. I ask professors to announce the event in their classes and pass around a sign-up sheet for names and phone numbers. The day before the practice conference, my students call the college students to remind them of the time and place and give any needed directions to the school.

On the day of the practice conference, the students and I prepare a buffet lunch. The college students arrive at noon, and I arrange to meet with them before they meet the students. I give them a little background about student-parent conferences. I explain that they will be playing the role of parents and are to ask "parent" questions during the conference. I also ask them to write about the experience before they leave for the day. During lunch, my students and the college students eat, chat, and get comfortable with each other. After cleanup, each college student is paired with one of my students and we begin. Normally, there are more sixth graders than college students, so I take the rest of my students out in the hall to silently read while conferences take place in the room. As one of my students finishes, another sixth grader takes her place. By 2:30, the college students are gone and we discuss the day. I ask my students to do a short reflective fast-write on the practice conference, thinking about what went well and anything they need to change. At a class meeting, we share successes and brainstorm possible solutions to those things that students want to improve. Now they are ready for the student-parent conference.

Conference Day
By the time conference day arrives, all the hard work is finished and I sigh with relief that we completed everything on track. Scheduling, food, music, and the physical environment are the finishing details that create a relaxing evening.

Scheduling
I initially began thinking that time was a major consideration in scheduling student-parent conferences. The first time, I scheduled the conferences during the school district's allotted time period. Since students only attend a half of the day during that week, it meant that the student-parent conferences would be held in the afternoons. While it was manageable within this time frame, I discovered some problems. Since many of my parents came to the conferences from work, they had to go home, pick up their child, and then come to school. Most parents only had a half hour to spend conferencing because they came during their lunch break. There just wasn't enough time if I kept the student-parent conferences during the day.

Barb Smith, a second-grade teacher at North Pole Elementary, has solved the time problem by scheduling her student-parent conferences at the end of the regular school conference day. The parents can attend conferences for other children and then end up in Barb's room for a leisurely and uninterrupted conference with their second grader.

The following quarter, I scheduled the conferences on a Tuesday evening. I was worried about having enough space if all the families showed up at one time, so I asked parents to sign up for a specific forty-five minute time slot. The conferences ran from 6:30 to 8:30, which worked much better than the day conferences. The parents didn't seem rushed, more parental pairs were able to come, and the students seemed more relaxed.

Now I always schedule the conferences in the evening. And I find I don't need to have families sign up for a specific time; they simply come any time between 6:30 and 8:00 (I moved up the end time so I wouldn't still be at school past 9:00). I believe the open scheduling adds to the relaxed feeling of the evening. Parents aren't worried about being late and the families can take their time and enjoy the evening together. My fear of not having enough space has proven unfounded. Somehow it all works out. If there isn't a desk open immediately, students give their family a tour of the room or offer refreshments.

The Physical Environment

Moving desks becomes our transition between practice and the real event. The students and I move about half the desks out into the hall to make room for families. The other desks are scattered around the room and spaced far enough apart to allow for both extra chairs and an element of privacy. To soften the classroom look, each desk is covered with a small tablecloth. Each desk also has a pen for signing the report card when the conference is over.

Food. Another group of students arranges the refreshments for the evening by placing cookies on a tray and mixing punch. They also create a serving area, cover it with a tablecloth, and create a centerpiece. Some of my classes have made their own refreshments such as cookies, muffins, and bread. One quarter we studied the history of Alaska so we made Alaskan food such as blueberry muffins and sourdough bread. This generated a lot of excitement with the students, but I don't bake with every class. I let refreshments depend on the particular class, our schedule, and my energy at the time.

Music. Music is the final part of the physical environment. It's another relaxing element that softens the institutional feeling and acts as a buffer between conversations at each desk. Soft classical music also helps everyone to slow down. For this evening, there are no time restrictions; taking time is important.

The Day After the Conferences

Time enters our discussion the day after the conferences as I meet with any student who didn't attend the night before. The student and family can arrange to have the conference before or after school or during lunch. Since I don't need to be in constant attendance, the time and place can be quite flexible. I do request that the first-quarter conference be done at school as it sets the tone for all the others, but after that the student can take the portfolio home and do the conference there if it's easiest for the parents. I don't encourage this as I find that there are too many interruptions at home that take away the focus from the student.

Each time we finish student-parent conferences, I think about all that we've accomplished. All twenty-eight students prepared and organized portfolios and successfully led conferences. I'm amazed that we do really it. Now the conference portfolios are stored in the cabinet to be used at the end of the year. New classroom portfolios sit on the shelf. Dale wrote, "I feel it [student-parent conference] is a cinch and I can do it again." The process begins anew.

Bibliography

Atwell, N. 1987. *In the Middle.* Portsmouth, NH: Heinemann.

Au, K., and A. Kawakami. 1985. "Research Currents: Talk Story and Learning to Read." *Language Arts* 62, no. 4 (April).

Blake, R., J. Mouton, and R. Allen. 1987. *Spectacular Teamwork— How to Develop the Leadership Skills for Team Success.* New York: John Wiley & Sons.

Brown, R. 1991. *Schools of Thought.* San Francisco: Jossey-Bass Publishers.

Covey, S. 1989. *The Seven Habits of Highly Effective People.* New York: Simon & Schuster.

Dewey, J. 1938. *Experience and Education.* New York: Macmillan Co.

Dias, P. 1989, June. Presentation at the Alaska Whole Language Institute, Fairbanks, Alaska.

"Equals, Programs in Mathematics, Technology, and Career Education." 1990, October. Course sponsored by the University of California, Berkeley: Lawrence Hall of Science. Held in Fairbanks, Alaska.

Goodlad, J. 1984. *A Place Called School.* New York: McGraw-Hill.

Graves, D. 1983. *Writing: Teachers and Children at Work.* Portsmouth, NH: Heinemann.

Harp, B., ed. 1991. *Assessment and Evaluation in Whole Language Programs.* Norwood, MA: Christopher-Gordon Publishers.

Johnson, D., & R. Johnson. 1984. *Motivational Processes in*

Cooperative, Competitive, and Individualistic Learning Situations. Minneapolis: University of Minnesota.

———. 1987. *Cooperative, Competitive, and Individualistic Learning.* Englewood Cliffs, NJ: Prentice-Hall.

Johnson, T. 1989, December. "The Teaching of Writing." Presentation to the Fairbanks North Star Borough School District, Fairbanks, Alaska.

———. 1990, January. "Viewing Assessment." Presentation to the Fairbanks North Star Borough School District, Fairbanks, Alaska.

Moorman, C. and D. Dishon. 1983. Portage, MI: Personal Power Press.

Perrone, V., ed. 1991. *Expanding Student Assessment.* Alexandria, VA: Association for Supervision and Curriculum Development.

Rief, L. 1991. *Seeking Diversity.* Portsmouth, NH: Heinemann.

Routman, R. 1991. *Invitations: Changing as Teachers and Learners K–12.* Portsmouth, NH: Heinemann.

Smith, F. 1986. *Insult to Intelligence.* Portsmouth, NH: Heinemann.

Taylor, D., and C. Dorsey-Gaines. 1988. *Growing Up Literate.* Portsmouth, NH: Heinemann.

Vygotsky, L. 1978. *Mind in Society.* Ed. Micheal Cole, Vera John-Steiner, Sylvia Scribner, and Ellen Souberman. Cambridge: Harvard University Press.

Weaver, C. 1988. *Reading Process and Practice.* Portsmouth, NH: Heinemann.

———. 1990. *Understanding Whole Language: From Principles to Practice.* Portsmouth, NH: Heinemann.